GARDENING FOR WILDLIFE

George Pilkington

This book is the result of the author's many years of observation and experience of gardens and the wildlife which visits them.

While reading it you will become more aware of the animals and plants around you and will discover practical ways to encourage them into your garden.

Alfresco Books

First published in 1999 by *Alfresco Books*
7 Pineways, Appleton, Warrington, WA4 5EJ

A CIP record for this book is available from the British Library.

ISBN 1 873727 12 7

Cover - Gordon Firth

Line drawings - George Pilkington, Gordon Firth

Typeset and design - Jen Darling

Printing - MFP Design & Print

This book is dedicated to my long suffering wife Kate, our three daughters, Rachel, Adele and Carmel, and dog, Penny, who all share my garden with lots of other wildlife!

FOREWORD

When I built and planted the very first wildlife garden at Chelsea Flower Show, back in 1985, it caused quite a stir within the horticultural establishment. By contrast, a great many 'ordinary' gardeners seemed to love the idea that a garden could be beautiful, comfortable and provide a safe haven for the wildlife which so many of us enjoy.

Since then, gardening with nature has become more popular every year, until these days Chelsea is packed with foxgloves, bluebells and primroses, the garden centres are overflowing with nestboxes and birdfeeders, and Britain's biggest-selling garden magazine, the BBC's *Gardeners' World*, carries a garden wildlife feature every month, by popular demand.

When I first met George Pilkington, he was my local, on-the-beat policeman in Warrington — always keen to lean on the fence and chat about newts and dragonflies, and to swap wildlife gardening notes. I remember being taken to admire a glorious patch of colourful cornfield annuals in his garden, and proudly showing off the spawning toads in mine.

Now, George has captured his years of practical experience in this book and his enthusiasm comes shining through. This is not a manual for nature reserve managers. This is a gardening book. It is full of useful tips and sound advice, and I'm sure it will persuade even more people with gardens to give nature a helping hand.

We have over one million acres of private gardens in Britain. Follow George's advice and these could become the biggest nature reserve in the country, whilst also providing the most immediate pleasure to those of us who live in towns.

Chris Baines

CONTENTS

Part One

BIRDS

WHY FEED THE BIRDS?

Pleasure, interest, education and the sheer fascination of observing birds are some of the reasons why people feed birds.

By feeding the birds you will not only enhance and enrich your own life but will also help to ensure that many more birds survive to breed.

Research has shown that many farmland birds, and even some garden birds, are in serious and dramatic decline. In our efforts to increase our food supply we have unwittingly decreased that of wild birds.

The removal, destruction and mismanagement of hedges has deprived birds, not only of nesting areas, but also of vital food sources, such as berries and insects.

By using chemicals to kill insects, the weeds they lived on and the seeds the weeds would have produced means many farmland birds are literally starving to death.

The practice of leaving fields fallow over the winter months has mostly disappeared. Birds would forage in these fields for grain, weed seeds and insects.

Our efficient methods of harvesting, storing and handling cereal crops has deprived birds of another food source. (The chaffinch was so named because it searches the chaff for spilt grain and seeds.)

Sowing winter crops causes problems for some bird species looking for food, especially in early Spring, when growing crops create cold, damp conditions at ground level, which affects insects' food supply.

Birds know instinctively which foods to feed to their nestlings. Providing a supplementary food source allows adults to sustain themselves, then feed any live food they find to their nestlings.

For all these reasons gardens are becoming increasingly important for many bird species struggling to survive in the open countryside.

WHEN TO FEED THE BIRDS

... quite simply all year round.

Many people take our garden birds for granted but put out bread and kitchen scraps in the Winter, then stop feeding birds at the start of Spring, believing enough natural food is around by then.

Many birds, especially finches, rely on seeds as food. During late Spring and early Summer there is a shortage of these and many birds die of starvation.

In Winter many birds eat weed, flower and tree seeds. By Spring, these seeds have either rotted, been eaten, blown or washed away, or are growing into young plants, which are not yet producing seed.

Other birds lay their eggs to coincide with the flush of leaves on trees, especially oaks, which in turn are consumed by newly hatched caterpillars — a vital protein source for newly hatched nestlings. Inclement weather can delay this glut of caterpillars. A late frost, hail storm, cold weather or a prolonged rainy spell can wipe them out and chicks will die.

Supplementary foods will benefit new fledglings trying to cope with any unseasonal shortages of natural food due to weather trends or other factors.

As Spring approaches birds' thoughts turn to things other than food! Males have to establish a territory, defend it, (even build the nest in some cases), be a beautiful singer and look magnificent in their new, bright and colourful plumage! A poorly fed, bedraggled male will not be able to compete and will be driven away without a partner. The fitter the birds, the more nestlings there will be.

Peanuts, black sunflower seeds and mealworms have proved invaluable during this critical period. (See Appendix for suppliers.)

WHERE TO FEED THE BIRDS

By providing a variety of foods, at different heights, in a variety of feeders and a variety of places the widest variety of birds will be attracted to your garden.

Bird tables, feeders, ground hoppers, ground tables, patios, lawns, under bushes, in nooks, crannies and tree trunks, along fences, behind climbers — food can be placed in all these places for birds to find.

Site feeders away from overhanging branches, fences and other obstacles up which cats can climb. Feeders should all be securely fixed so that they do not blow off and injure birds feeding below.

Consider erecting a simple chicken wire cage around a piece of lawn or patio area. This will stop bigger birds from entering and eating all the food, and provide safety from predators.

Ground tables and hoppers have the advantage as they concentrate all the birds in one place, making viewing easier.

However, even in their continual search for food, birds, like the wren and goldcrest, rarely leave the cover of dense vegetation, such as ivy, hedgerows, bushes or conifers. And these shyer birds will appreciate food placed under hedges and trees, or in a quiet area of the garden.

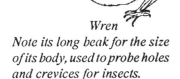

Wren
Note its long beak for the size of its body, used to probe holes and crevices for insects.

Peanut granules *are an ideal foodstuff to scatter under hedges as they will not germinate like the seeds in many mixtures.*

A bird will always choose natural supplies first. However, even the largest suburban gardens will quickly be stripped of these.

Nowadays, prepared foods from reputable companies have been formulated after years of research and experiments to provide the right balance for a healthy and nutritious diet.

Aflatoxin is a fungal growth that can affect peanuts and cereal crops. It can cause serious damage to the immune systems of birds and can even kill in severe cases.

The Birdfoods Standards Association (BSA) was set up some years ago to provide quality foods **guaranteed** aflatoxin free. Before buying, check that your seed supplier is a member and the food stocked bears the BSA logo.

To survive in the wild birds have to be in peak condition. Nature soon deals with the sick, the injured and the starving. A balanced intake of a range of foods is required. For instance, to evade predators birds need a quick boost of energy over a short period, while to fly any distance requires another form of energy.

Sunflower 'hearts' are a newcomer to bird feeding. The 'heart' is the seed without its husk — an excellent foodstuff and an improvement on the already highly successful black sunflower seed. (This has a thinner shell and higher oil and protein content than the ordinary, black-and-white sunflower seed.)

A BALANCED DIET

Birds need:

Fat—for insulation, energy, vitamins and to balance bodily functions.
Found in: coconut, nuts, peanuts, meat, bacon rind, cheese, cakes, biscuits and pastry.

> *Peanut granules are the growing tips of peanuts and are richer in oil and protein than the rest of the peanut. Many birds will eat these.*

Protein — for many vital functions, such as the growth and repair of cells and body maintenance.
Found in: nuts, cereals, cheese, meat and poultry scraps, mealworms and cooked potatoes.

Carbohydrates — for the main energy supply, needed for quick bursts, endurance and future reserves.
Found in: bread, pasta, cooked potatoes, fresh and dried fruits, berries and cereals.

Minerals and Vitamins — the cornerstones of a healthy, strong body, preventing deficiency diseases and performing specific functions throughout the body and nervous system.
Found in: mixed seeds, meat, nuts, cooked potatoes, cereals, cheese, fruit and berries.

> *Cereals include oats, oatmeal, maize, millet and wheat, which can all be found in the better quality mixed bird foods, usually mixed with various small seeds.*

Water — vital for drinking and maintaining healthy feathers. The digestive system, the passing of waste products and the lubricating of bones and eyes all need water too.

WHAT BIRDS LIKE TO EAT

Species	Supplementary Food	Site
Blackbird and Robin	bread, cake, biscuits, oatmeal, chips, fat, grated cheese, worms, mealworms, berries, apples, sultanas, peanut granules.	G/T
Blackcap	berries, roast potato, fat.	G/T
Chaffinch	mixed seed, peanut granules, oatmeal.	G/T
Collared Dove	bread, cake, biscuits, oatmeal, chips, peanuts, seeds and sunflower seeds (eaten whole!), berries.	G/T
Dunnock	small mixed seeds, peanut granules, breadcrumbs, oatmeal, porridge, mealworms.	G
Feral Pigeon	bread, cake, chips, grain, oatmeal, seeds.	G/T
Fieldfare and Mistle Thrush	berries, apples and crab apples, pears, sultanas, worms and meal worms.	G
Finches - bull, green and gold	Small, mixed seeds, peanut granules, sunflower hearts and seeds.	G/T/F
Heron	Prized fish! Tadpoles, frogs.	G
House Sparrow	bread, biscuits, oatmeal, porridge, grain, fat, scraps, peanuts/granules, sunflower seeds.	G/T/F
Jackdaw Crow, Magpie	Bread, fat, meat scraps, kitchen scraps, mealworms.	G/T
Jay	whole peanuts, acorns	G/T
Kestrels and Sparrowhawks	garden birds!	G/T
Nuthatch	peanuts, sunflower seeds, grated cheese, fat.	G/T/F/Tr

Species	Supplementary Food	Site
Pheasant	grain, seeds, bread, oatmeal, kitchen scraps.	G/T
Pied Wagtail	mixed seeds, peanut granules, oatmeal, bread crumbs, mealworms.	G
Redwing	berries, apples and crab apples, pears, worms and mealworms.	G
Reed Bunting	mixed seeds, peanut granules, breadcrumbs.	G/T
Siskins	peanuts, small seeds, fat.	G/T
Song Thrush	as redwing, plus sunflower hearts (seed without husk).	G
Starlings	peanuts/granules, apples, pears, oatmeal, bread, cake, biscuits, chips, meat scraps, fat, kitchen scraps.	G/T/F
Tit family	coconut, peanuts/granules, small seeds, sunflower seeds, breadcrumbs, grated cheese, suet, fat, meat scraps, mealworms.	G/T/F
Tree Creeper	fat, suet, mealworms, wedged peanuts/nuts in trees and shrubs.	T/Tr
Tree Sparrow	bread, seeds, peanuts/granules, mealworms.	G/T/F
Woodpecker	peanuts, fat, suet, mealworms.	Tr/T/F
Wood Pigeon	bread, seeds, berries, peas, brassica leaves.	G
Wren and Goldcrest	mealworms, grated cheese, fat, oatmeal, breadcrumbs, peanut granules.	C

Preferred Feeding Sites

G - Ground   F - Feeder
T - Table   Tr - Tree Trunk
C - Areas with Cover

THE PERFECT BIRD FEEDER

What to look for when buying and using a feeder:

Some bird feeders are badly designed; some are dangerous for birds to use. The best bird feeder will be specially designed for birds and not just to please humans.

Quality feeders from reputable companies are more expensive but bird safety will be paramount in their design and manufacture. (See list in Appendix.)

Questions to ask:

Is the feeder made of rustproof metal?

Has it been coated with toxic metals?

Can a bird injure itself because the mesh is too large or too small?

Can squirrels chew through it?

Is the top weatherproof and easily opened for filling?

Is the base angled for birds to reach the food easily?

Are there drainage holes?

Can the base be easily cleaned?

Can an optional pole be fitted?

Ensure that feeders are filled with the food for which they are designed. Never fill them with wild birdseed or cereal mixes.

SUNFLOWER AND PEANUT FEEDERS

Peanut Feeder

Some processes used to coat metal mesh in zinc oxide can leave toxic residue on nuts. Buy steel or non-toxic coated mesh feeders.

Mesh size too large - whole nut can be removed; too small - bird may damage beak.

Some badly designed peanut feeders have trapped birds' legs, causing injury and even death.

Do not fill with mixed seed, which may contain cereals which can get wet, mouldy and clog up your feeder. Birds will select the choicest food, the rest will rot in the feeder.

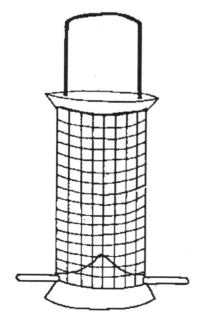

Sunflower Seed Feeder

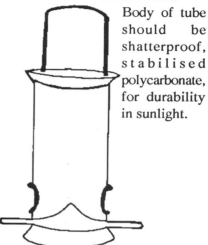

Body of tube should be shatterproof, stabilised polycarbonate, for durability in sunlight.

Feeding ports should be offset on feeders with more than 2 ports, to allow birds to feed in peace and not feel threatened by other birds feeding too close.

Feeding ports with holes too large - a bird could trap its head; too small - it could hurt itself trying to reach food, or it might not be able to remove food at all.

Feeding ports with slight lips help prevent rain wetting the food.

Do not fill with cereal based, mixed birdseed or peanuts. They can stop the smooth flow of sunflower seeds in the feeder and, in the case of mixed seed, clog the feeder with unwanted food.

SAFETY FIRST FOR BIRDS

REMEMBER — THINK BIRD SAFETY

Safety for the birds is a responsibility we owe to them if we wish to attract them into our garden to feed.

Securely fix your hanging feeder by cutting a 9 cm length of metal coathanger and shaping it into an 'S'.

A falling feeder could be badly damaged and might injure ground feeding birds.

Hang your feeders on a washing-free(!) line. They will be out of reach of cats and not as easily blown off as hanging from a tree.

All bird feeders, hoppers, tables and patios should be cleaned **regularly** with a mild disinfectant. Diseases are **easily** transmitted when birds congregate in small areas, especially in large numbers.

By providing peanuts in safe, well designed peanut feeders we act responsibly and eliminate the possibility of nestlings choking on whole peanuts.

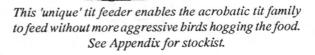

This 'unique' tit feeder enables the acrobatic tit family to feed without more aggressive birds hogging the food. See Appendix for stockist.

BIRD TABLES

What sort of table?

Bird tables allow us to observe birds at eye level. Not all birds will use them; some prefer to feed on the ground.

Keep your table clean and safe for the birds. If you use a wood preservative make sure it is environmentally friendly.

No overhanging branches or obstacles should be near, from which cats can pounce on unsuspecting birds.

Place your bird table where you can see it and not too far from your kitchen door. You are more likely to keep it topped up the nearer it is to your house, especially if it snows!

Ground Tables

These are a relatively new idea. They are basic wooden tables, several centimetres off the ground and with a stainless steel mesh floor.

Water easily drains through the mesh floor, keeping food reasonably dry. A raised wooden edge prevents food from being blown off.

This table is easy to clean.

It can be moved around the garden easily, so lessening the risk of disease from dirty feeding areas.

A simple wire cage can be erected around it for added safety.

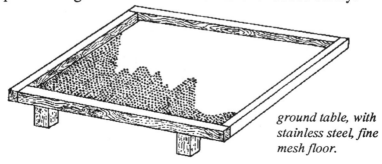

ground table, with stainless steel, fine mesh floor.

THE BEST BIRD TABLE

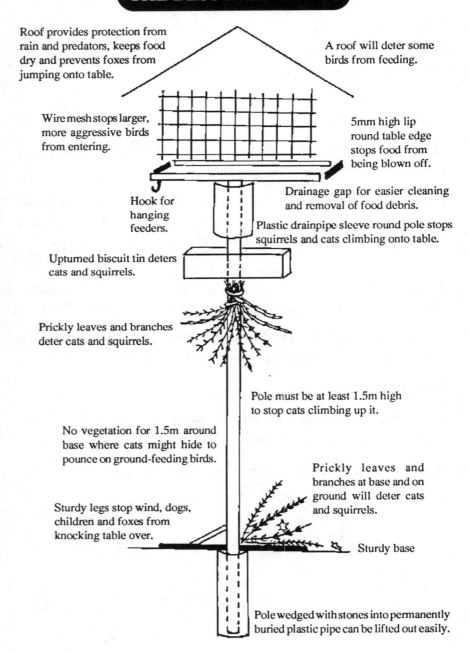

Roof provides protection from rain and predators, keeps food dry and prevents foxes from jumping onto table.

A roof will deter some birds from feeding.

Wire mesh stops larger, more aggressive birds from entering.

5mm high lip round table edge stops food from being blown off.

Hook for hanging feeders.

Drainage gap for easier cleaning and removal of food debris.

Plastic drainpipe sleeve round pole stops squirrels and cats climbing onto table.

Upturned biscuit tin deters cats and squirrels.

Prickly leaves and branches deter cats and squirrels.

Pole must be at least 1.5m high to stop cats climbing up it.

No vegetation for 1.5m around base where cats might hide to pounce on ground-feeding birds.

Prickly leaves and branches at base and on ground will deter cats and squirrels.

Sturdy legs stop wind, dogs, children and foxes from knocking table over.

Sturdy base

Pole wedged with stones into permanently buried plastic pipe can be lifted out easily.

DO'S AND DON'TS

DO ...

Keep your bird food in vermin proof containers.

Put out fresh food daily and provide for ground feeders, tree trunk feeders and acrobats! — for example, dunnocks, nuthatches and tits.

Provide a wide variety of food in a wide variety of places and feeders.

Provide a safe environment for birds to feed in safety from predators and diseases.

Site tables, feeders and hoppers to give all round vision — at least 1.5 metres from ground vegetation, but with nearby cover for escape .

Clean your feeders, hoppers, tables and patios regularly with a mild disinfectant. Many birds congregating in a small area allows disease to spread easily from faecal and spittle deposits from birds already infected. Wear gloves when cleaning.

Change the ground feeding areas of your garden regularly — to minimise the risk of disease

Take time to observe the antics of wild bird visitors.

Cut up bacon rind, or tie it onto a washing line. Birds can choke on large pieces of rind.

Smash peanuts into fragments. More bird species can eat small pieces than can tackle a whole peanut — and the peanuts last longer!

Use a washing line rather than hanging feeders in trees. Cats can't walk along it.

Use a metal coat hanger. Cut a piece 9 cms long and bend it into an S shape. Hang your feeder from this.

Soak bread, oats and cake in fat from your grill pan — to make it more nutritious.

DO ...

Soak bread in water. It stops birds from choking on hard pieces, lets more birds eat it and stops larger birds taking all the big pieces.

Place a small mat or carpet on the ground prior to snow or frost. Remove it later to give the birds a clear area from which to feed.

On bare, open areas in your garden push conifer prunings into the ground to create instant hedges. They will attract hedge-loving birds and, if planted densely enough, will create snow-free pockets, give cover and shelter from the elements and encourage shy birds to feed.

If you have a rowan tree in your garden or street, sweep up windfall berries early in the season (which are generally wasted), place in your freezer and use in Winter, when natural sources are exhausted.

Collect a few large bags of leaves (or make leaf mould) and scatter these under hedges, bushes and trees to create a more natural environment for woodland birds to forage for insects.

See where birds forage. Put fat, grated cheese and mealworms there.

Dip the tips of branches, flower heads and ivy stems in melted fat.

Smear cheese and fat along branches and wooden fences. Wedge peanuts into tree trunks. Be imaginative! The birds certainly are when they forage.

Put out mealworms, waxworms and earthworms. They provide a valuable source of protein, will be eaten by a huge variety of birds and can be used safely all year — in prepacked tubs for the squeamish! (See Appendix for suppliers.)

Drill a silver birch log with holes. Fill them with fat and/or peanuts, then hang from a tree.

Provide fresh water daily.

Remember, I like birds too.

Buy an electronic cat deterrent.

DON'T ...

Buy a bird table with a nest incorporated. Birds may not tolerate other birds feeding on their doorstep. Predatory birds will be attracted too.

Feed desiccated coconut, uncooked rice or pasta (which can swell up inside a bird), salted peanuts or hot curry! Birds like cheese but not Danish blue!

Put poultry carcasses on the floor; they may attract vermin. Use a taut washing line.

Use seeds that are too old or of poor quality.

Overface your birds with too much food. Other than in feeders, no food should be left by the evening; it attracts rats. If you do have food left check whether this is for one of the reasons mentioned above.

Forget to top up your feeders and provide fresh water daily.

Buy cheap bird food which doesn't bear the logo of the Birdfood Standard Association.

Place your feeders, tables, etc. where cats can pounce.

Stop feeding once you start. Although not totally dependent on you your feeding station does form a critical part of a bird's feeding cycle. The longer and colder nights mean a bird uses up more fat reserves just to keep warm. Less daylight hours mean less time to look for and find enough food to replace this fat. Quite simply there may not be enough time for a bird to find an alternative food source to the one you created and the bird may die, especially on a very cold night.

A Tip ...
Plastic paint trays make ideal bird baths, their shallow end encouraging the smaller birds to drink and bathe.

DON'T ...

Thread peanuts in their kernels. The time wasted and eventual energy gained by a bird working on opening a kernel may not replace the time and energy gained from its contents. Use a feeder instead.

Feed whole peanuts, especially early in the breeding season when inexperienced fledglings are learning to survive alone. Use a feeder.

Put unsuitable food into your bird feeders.

Dead head your flowers. They may well provide seed, or resting places for insects, which birds can find and eat.

goldfinch with seed

Place your birdbaths, feeders and tables too far from the kitchen door. In cold weather will you venture out to replenish them if they are a distance away?

Although you could entice birds which eat acorns, hazelnuts and beechmast into your garden by collecting these from the wild, do leave this natural food supply for birds to eat there, or you could deplete an already dwindling food source. Peanuts are an excellent substitute.

WHERE BIRDS NEST

With fewer trees and hedgerows, and more and more manicured and tidy gardens, many birds, especially those using holes, nooks and crannies, are finding it difficult to find suitable nesting sites.

To increase numbers, no matter how well fed they are, birds need nesting sites. With a little thought and planning gardens can provide many bird species with suitable places to nest.

A combination of tall trees, thick, dense hedges, nesting boxes and suitable crevices or holes, could well provide for several different species to nest in the same garden.

Birds prefer natural sites, such as hollows in trees, ivy-covered walls, thick, prickly hedges, or trees and areas of dense vegetation. Have you any in your garden?

Affix wooden shelves onto wooden fencing, sheds or walls at various heights, then plant climbers, such as ivy or honeysuckle, at the base, with netting to help the climber to climb.

Leave a window open in your garage or shed. It may attract robins, wrens or even swallows to nest there.

If safe to do so, leave a dead tree or two in situ. Woodpeckers may well take up residence in them.

Basically, two types of nesting sites are used by garden nesting birds. The 'open' nesters — blackbirds, finches, thrushes — usually nest in trees, hedges and dense vegetation, although blackbirds have been known to use shelves in garden sheds!

The 'crevice and hole' nesters — wrens, blue tits, robins — find sites in trees, houses and sheds, or an almost limitless list of other sites, including overcoats, kettles, letter boxes and metal gate posts.

BIRD BOXES

If we invite birds to nest in our gardens it is our duty to protect them and their offspring from predators and the worst of the weather.

Nest boxes should be predator- and weather- proof, be able to breathe and offer good insulation properties. Cold or damp weather and predators kill off many nestlings and fledglings.

Wooden nest boxes have been used successfully by birds for generations. They have good insulation and breathability properties, are relatively cheap and easy to make.

Ensure the wood is at least 2 cms thick. This offers better insulation. A vertical grain assists the rain to run off. Raise the floor slightly to allow this to happen and so that water doesn't seep underneath. Put a few, small drainage holes in the floor.

Check the wood for cracks, splits and holes. **All** joints should be waterproof **and** draughtproof. Many birds die due to cold draughts. Use waterproof glue. A baton at the back will angle the box forward slightly and offer some rain protection.

Rustic boxes soon start to rot when the bark falls off. Use seasoned wood, with environmentally-friendly wood preservative **on the outside only**.

Iron nails and screws can rust and make wood rot. Use galvanised or brass screws. Screws give a better draughtproof seal than nails as they pull the sides together.

Check old nesting boxes for holes, splits, cracks or warping.

Plastic pipes can suffer from condensation and have poor insulating properties. The rigid, double-skinned, ribbed drainage pipes, with a wooden floor and wooden roof, have proved more successful.

Metal boxes should be placed in the shade to prevent overheating.

The roof should have an all-round overhang, with at least a 2.5 cm canopy over the entrance hole. The roof should be tight fitting and removable or hinged.

Wood crete boxes, made from a mixture of sawdust, concrete and burnt clay, are proving very successful for nesting birds. These are completely rot proof, weather and predator resistant, with excellent thermal and breathability properties. (See Appendix for suppliers.)

Decide which birds you want to nest. The entrance hole should be 2.5 cms for blue tits, 2.8 cms for great tits — any larger and sparrows, or even starlings, will occupy the nest.

Robins nest in open-fronted boxes.

robin

Nesting Material

Provide nesting material, such as carpet fluff, wool, animal hairs, dried leaves, twigs, moss, dried grass, cottonwool and mud. Make little piles on the ground and see which birds take which material.

The cheap, plastic peanut feeders make excellent nesting material dispensers. Pack the above materials in and tease strands out of the holes for birds to take away.

LOOKING AFTER YOUR BIRD BOX

When the birds have left it is important to open a nestbox and clean it out. There may be dead birds or unhatched eggs inside. There will certainly be fleas, lice and parasites in the nesting material, awaiting their next host.

In late Autumn remove any dead birds, then place the nest in the microwave and cook on high for 20 seconds. This should kill any parasites and their eggs.

Disinfect the box by washing it in hot, soapy water.

Replace the nest in the box. With luck the birds will re-use it next year, will have less work to do and it will be parasite-free.

As an alternative, add a few vegetables and make birds nest soup with the cooked nest!

Do return your bird box to its site. Birds use them to roost in, especially during the cold, winter months. The nesting material will add insulation to the box, keeping them warm in Winter and in Spring, saving them spending time and energy finding material to build a new nest.

SITE AND POSITION

Site boxes out of direct sunlight. Use the drier side of a tree. Siting the entrance hole north to south-east is arguably the most favourable aspect if no shelter is available. The hole should face light.

Site tit boxes at least 1.5 metres above the ground, for ease of cleaning and out of reach of cats. They should be securely fixed so as not to be blown or knocked down. Fix them to posts or trees, using wire, not nails, inside a bike's inner tube, so as not to damage the tree.

Do not site near a feeding area or bird table. The site should provide protection from wind, rain and unseasonal hailstones. A sheltered, quiet area is best.

Bird boxes are available for installing into existing or newly built buildings. These are ideal for those living in urban areas. (See Appendix for stockist.)

A wigwam of metal or wooden poles is easy to construct. Planting climbers to grow up this, then placing a bird box near the top could encourage a bird to nest there, especially when overgrown.

Hide your bird box from predators.

PREDATOR PROOF

Perches are not needed by nesting birds and can allow a predator to gain a foothold. The entrance hole should be at least 12 cms from the bottom of the nest, to make it more difficult for nestlings to be taken.

Beware of cats. Boxes fixed to the top of wooden fences, garages, etc. are within easy reach and overhanging branches offer a perch from which cats can pounce.

Woodpeckers enlarge entrance holes and corner joints in wooden boxes to prey on nestlings. Deter them with metal or rubber strips around these vulnerable areas, or purchase a wood crete box.

Placing bird boxes on wooden poles with a collar of bramble, rose or gorse wrapped round the pole, will deter cats and squirrels, or you can use a metal pole.

Secure holly leaves or hawthorn cuttings on the roof of a box to deter predators from landing there. Also ensure that the roof cannot be easily removed by either predators or gales, leaving the nestlings vulnerable to both wily animals and the weather.

A protective 'bubble' of chicken wire around nest boxes, in place before nesting occurs, can offer some protection from predators.

Conceal open-fronted boxes in dense vegetation or in thick, thorny trees or hedges. Use prickly collars both above and below boxes on tree trunks.

Get a dog, or a neutered tom cat with a bell the size of Big Ben attached to a collar!

CLIMBERS FOR BIRDS

Species	Growth	Insects	Fruit	Seed
*Bramble	Very fast	Yes	Yes	-

Comments: Good for nesting. Thorny. Good for butterflies. Grow in full sun for better flowers and fruit.

Species	Growth	Insects	Fruit	Seed
*Dog Rose	Fast	Yes	Yes	-

Comments: Likes sun. Good for nesting. Thorny. Good in a hedge.

Species	Growth	Insects	Fruit	Seed
*Wild Ivy	Fast	Yes	Yes	-

Comments: Excellent year round cover. Berries in late Winter.

Species	Growth	Insects	Fruit	Seed
*Sweet Briar	Fast	Yes	Yes	-

Comments: Pretty flowers. Good for nesting. Good in a hedge.

Species	Growth	Insects	Fruit	Seed
*Field Rose	Fast	Yes	Yes	-

Comments: Later flowers than dog rose. Good for nesting. Good in hedge.

Species	Growth	Insects	Fruit	Seed
*Wild Honeysuckle	Very Fast	Yes	Yes	-

Comments: Moths and bees like it. Lovely perfume. Semi-evergreen. Good cover. Some berries.

Species	Growth	Insects	Fruit	Seed
Clematis	Moderate	-	-	-

Comments: Lovely flowers. Good cover. (Non-native)

Species	Growth	Insects	Fruit	Seed
Russian Vine	Very Fast	-	-	-

Comments: Useful for cover only. (Non-native)

Species	Growth	Insects	Fruit	Seed
Travellers Joy	Very Fast	Yes	-	Yes

Comments: Good cover. Rampant.

* Recommended

For their seeds, grow lavender, teasels, sunflowers and knapweed, which some birds, especially goldfinches, love.

IVY

Ivy must be one of the most beneficial and underrated plants for wildlife. Contrary to popular belief it does not kill trees by strangulation or sap them of energy like a parasite seeking the juices of its host.

Ivy has its own extensive root system and can use up the sun's energy to photosynthesise (make its own food) like most other plants. The only time ivy may be a problem is to a very old or diseased tree when its weight may cause a dying branch to fall off.

Many birds nest in it, feeding on insects that dwell in and around it. Wrens, for instance, love hunting amongst ivy. It provides shelter for birds, mammals and insects, not only from inclement weather but also from the hot, midday sun.

Butterflies, such as the brimstone, hibernate amongst its leaves, as do many other insects in Winter. The holly blue butterfly lays its eggs on the developing flower buds and berries, which its caterpillars eat before they hibernate as a chrysalis.

The ivy's late autumn flowers attract the last of the butterflies and flying insects to feed on their nectar.

The berries are a valuable source of food for birds in the depth of Winter, when most other berries have been depleted.

Planted as described here, a bare wooden fence, brick wall or garden shed will quickly be covered, providing a screen and a useful vertical habitat for wildlife.

Ivy is one of the best plants for a wildlife garden.

IVY — PERFECT PLANTING

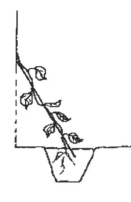

This shows a typical method of planting ivy next to a wooden fence or brick wall. Most wooden fences have a concrete base. Both brick and concrete absorb moisture away from the ivy, making this area very dry and extremely difficult for the ivy to get established.

Note the garden centre support cane slanting towards the wall in the vain hope that the ivy will climb it and then grow up the wall. Ivy produces little suckers on **new** growth and it's these new suckers (not the old growth) which cling to the wall. So they need to be encouraged.

A better method of planting is to dig a small trench at least 30 cms from the wall, 60 cms and 30 cms wide, to a spade's depth.

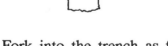

Fork into the trench as far as possible, breaking up all the subsoil. Incorporate and work into the soil some organic matter — garden compost, manure or leaf mould. This will retain moisture and encourage the roots to grow.

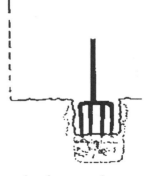

fence

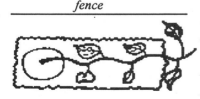

After planting the ivy to the same depth as it was in the container, filling in the trench and firming the soil, lay the ivy plant either to the right (as in the diagram) or to the left.

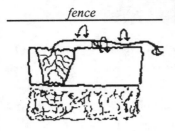

fence

Make several u-shaped pins (a wire coat hanger is ideal for this) and use them to pin the ivy stem to the ground. The stem **must** come into contact with the soil for the roots to grow.

This shows the plant sitting on top of the manured and forked area of the trench, with the pins about to be inserted.

Leave the growth facing the fence but cut **all** the rest, including the top.

This shows the growth a year after planting.

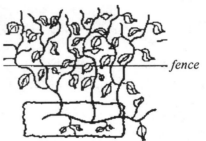

fence

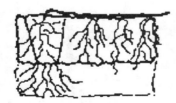

This shows the extent of the original (potted) root system and the new root system of the plant, which has increased tremendously and will boost the growth of the plant.

This shows how to cut the growth after the first year. This will encourage all the new growth to send out many more side shoots, covering a far more extensive area.

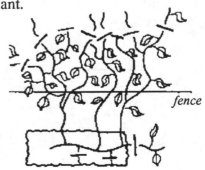

fence

GARDEN TREES AND SHRUBS FOR BIRDS

Trees provide song and lookout posts, shelter, food, nesting sites and nesting material.

The oak is the king of trees for birds, insects and mammals. Plant acorns in a hedge, then prune the saplings to a manageable height.

Before planting trees consideration should be given to their eventual size. A good tree identification book will give this information.

Species	Growth	Insects	Fruit	Seed	Coppice	Hedge
Alder	Average	Yes	-	Yes	Yes	-

Comments: Will grow in damp conditions. Goldfinches and siskins love the seed.

Barberry	Average	Yes	Yes	-	-	Yes

Comments: Thorny. Good for nesting. Many varieties.

Bird Cherry	Average	Yes	Yes	-	-	-

Comments: A smaller tree than wild cherry.

Blackthorn	Fast	Yes	Yes	-	-	Yes

Comments: Very early flowers. Thorny. Good for nesting.

Buckthorn	Average	Yes	Yes	-	-	Yes

Comments: Food plant for the brimstone butterfly larva.

Cherry (wild)	Average	Yes	Yes	-	-	Yes

Comments: Flowers early (earlier than bird cherry).

Cotoneaster	Average	Few	Yes	-	-	Yes

Comments: Excellent for bumble bees. Many species of plant.

Crab Apple	Average	VG	Yes	-	-	-

Comments: Pollinator for apples. John Downie is better than Golden Hornet.

Downy Birch	Fast	VG	-	Yes	Yes	-

Comments: Will grow in damp areas. Casts light shade. Moth larvae.

Elderberry	Fast	Few	VG	-	Yes	-

Comments: Both flowers and fruit. Makes excellent wine!

Species	Growth	Insects	Fruit	Seed	Coppice	Hedge
Field Maple	Average	Few	-	-	Yes	Yes
Guelder Rose	Average	Yes	Yes	-	Yes	Yes
Hawthorn	Fast	VG	Yes	-	Yes	Yes
Hazel	Slow	Yes	-	Nuts	Yes	Yes
Holly	Slow	Few	Yes	-	Yes	Yes
Hornbeam	Slow	Few	-	-	Yes	Yes
Pussy Willow	Very Fast	VG	-	-	Yes	Yes
Pyracantha	Average	Few	VG	-	Yes	Yes
Rowan	Average	Yes	VG	-	-	-
Silver Birch	Fast	VG	-	Yes	Yes	-
Spindle	Very Fast	Yes	-	-	-	-
Wayfaring	Average	-	Yes	-	-	-
Whitebeam	Average	Few	VG	-	-	-
Wild Privet	Fast	Yes	Yes	-	Yes	Yes
Yew	Very Slow	Few	Yes	-	-	Yes

Comments (Field Maple): Will grow on clay.

Comments (Guelder Rose): Will grow in damp areas. Good for hoverflies.

Comments (Hawthorn): Thorny. Good for nesting. Moth larvae.

Comments (Hazel): Good for both mammals and birds.

Comments (Holly): A thorny evergreen. Holly Blue butterflies.

Comments (Hornbeam): Keeps leaves in Winter. Good cover. Good in a hedge.

Comments (Pussy Willow): Excellent for insects and small birds.

Comments (Pyracantha): This will grow up a wall. Firethorn is a good variety.

Comments (Rowan): Early berries.

Comments (Silver Birch): Casts light shade. Moth larvae.

Comments (Spindle): Has flowers and unique berries.

Comments (Wayfaring): Has flowers and berries.

Comments (Whitebeam): Excellent berries

Comments (Wild Privet): Butterfly and insect nectar. Small thorns.

Comments (Yew): Evergreen. Good for nesting.

Part Two

BUTTERFLIES

ABOUT BUTTERFLIES

The lack of flowers and nectar-rich weeds makes the countryside a very inhospitable place for butterflies and many species are declining.

Butterflies indicate what the natural and local environment is like. They abound in chemical-free areas where there are wildflowers and hedgerows to attract them.

Butterflies form part of the food chain, especially as caterpillars for insect-eating birds.

Their beauty and elusive flight make them a pleasure to watch as they flit from flower to flower, sipping nectar and pollinating flowers as they travel.

Gardens become increasingly important for butterflies as they stock up with nectar on their journey to find a mate.

Nectar is needed as their main source of energy and is vital for them prior to mating.

Some species will hibernate in garden sheds, garages and houses.

Central heating can prematurely awaken hibernating butterflies, which will then head for the window in an attempt to go outside.

The cold weather will kill them, so gently catch the butterfly and place cotton wool soaked in glucose near it. (Glucose is best as sugar or honey can crystallise in its proboscis.) Let it replace its energy and build up its reserves before placing it in an outdoor shed or garage.

ATTRACTING BUTTERFLIES

Where you live, the soil type, local factors, the proximity to different wildlife habitats and the weather, will all determine which species will visit your garden.

By planting at least part of your garden with nectar-rich plants in a sun trap, making a nectar oasis, will entice butterflies to stay longer than just a passing visit.

Butterflies prefer hot, sunny, sheltered areas in the garden to feed and bask. Plan your planting to achieve this, with short plants at the front and taller ones at the rear.

It is essential to remove all weeds by hand, not by chemical means, prior to planting. A hedged border to the north is an ideal background.

Concentrate on planting the recommended plants in large, bold patches, the larger the better, rather than planting in small numbers.

Butterflies are attracted by strong scents and large visible displays. Some will feed on over-ripened fruit and honeydew from aphids (greenfly).

In Autumn put rotten plums, damsons, apples and pears on your lawn.

Mix nectar-rich wild flowers and garden cultivars in your sheltered, nectar oasis.

Plant annuals at the front of the border. They are easier to remove from there before replanting.

Position plants of similar heights together. Butterflies have difficulty landing on flowers that are obstructed by higher plants, especially in breezy weather.

Provide nectar from Spring through to late Autumn.

PLANTS RICH IN NECTAR

The following list of flowers and shrubs can all be used by either butterflies or moths for nectar. Others are used as well. They are listed in approximate flowering order, from Spring to late Autumn.

Late flowering Winter Heathers
* Primrose
Grape Hyacinth
* Dandelion
Aubretia
* Bugle
* Garlic Mustard
Honesty
* Dames Violet (Sweet Rocket)
* Forget-me-not
* Red Campion
Candytuft
Dahlia Coltness hybrids

Buddleia
Lavender
Privet (not golden)
* Devils Bit Scabious
* Teasels
* Hemp Agrimony
* Knapweeds
Brambles (Thornless are best!)
* Fleabane (pulicaria vulgaris)
Sedum Spectabile (**not** named varieties)
Michaelmas Daisies
Ivy

* Wildflowers grown from seed.

—*proboscis*

Time to unwind and drink the amber nectar!

Butterflies and moths use a **proboscis** to drink nectar from within the flowers. Some have a shorter proboscis and are restricted in the flowers they can use. When not in use the proboscis is curled up like a watch spring.

BUTTERFLY BREEDING PLANTS

To encourage butterflies to breed in your garden requires exacting conditions. Most gardens do not create these conditions and if they are not met butterflies will not lay their eggs.

Micro-climate, plant variety and position, height and condition, are all assessed by the butterfly, both visually and using chemical sensors on its feet, antennae and body.

Small tortoiseshell, red admiral, peacock, painted lady and comma will all lay their eggs on nettles.

Cut nettles down in June to encourage fresh, young growth. Leave cut stems at the site for caterpillars already feeding on them.

Butterflies are unlikely to lay on an old nettle patch in a shady corner. Nettles in full sun and a sheltered position are better.

Garlic mustard, honesty, ladies smock and dames violet will attract the orange tip and green-veined white to lay.

Two shrub species of buckthorn (alder and purging) may attract a passing brimstone, while holly (female) and ivy attract the holly blue.

Hints and Tips
If you have more than one buddleia, prune them at different times in early Spring to extend the flowers. Also remove any dead flowers to encourage more side flowers.

Do not prune your privet but allow it to flower.

Train a thornless blackberry (in full sun) to grow up a wooden fence.

Hedges offer more wind protection and shelter than fences.

Create a sheltered nectar oasis in large bold patches.

Observe what plants butterflies are using at garden centres and in other gardens.

Part Three

BENEFICIAL WILDLIFE

Some well known and well loved species of beneficial wildlife appear in this section. Also included are less well known creatures which, through ignorance or fear, are often crushed underfoot. Hopefully, the information given will enable people to understand them better.

HEDGEHOGS

Being nocturnal, the only time many people see a hedgehog is when one has been killed on a road. If you are lucky enough to see one, or better still have one visit your garden, observing them and their antics makes an interesting, and sometimes amusing, pastime.

Their varied diet consists of earwigs, beetles, caterpillars, wood lice, worms, slugs, millipedes, birds' eggs and occasionally nestlings.

We should make our gardens as 'hedgehog friendly' as possible. Fibreglass and plastic ponds can become a death trap for hedgehogs who fall in, then drown because of the sheer, slippery slopes. Provide a bridge, perhaps using clematis wire, a wooden platform or stones for them to crawl up, then scamper out.

Plastic pea or bean netting, if left lying around, can entangle a hapless hedgehog and even kill it.

Provide nesting areas for Summer and Winter. Hedgehogs make nests in such places as undisturbed piles of dead leaves, log piles, compost heaps, old tree stumps, brushwood piles, under sheds, hedges, bramble patches and logs.

Hibernation sites are vital. They need to be dry, weatherproof and well insulated. A good site is useless without nesting material. Dry grass, straw, dry leaves and dry, shredded newspaper have all been used by hedgehogs in the past.

The hedgehog will collect and carry the material, stuff it into its chosen site, then turn round and round many times, until the nesting material forms a tight ball around its body, which is kept in place by the confines of the site.

Large gardens may have larger trees with hollows, rabbit holes and holes in banks. Stuff such places with dry nesting material. Nesting boxes for hedgehogs can also be bought. (See Appendix for stockists.)

BATS

Bats are attractive, small furry mammals and are under threat from lack of food and suitable sites in which to breed and roost. The use of insecticides and weedkillers is also reducing the numbers of insects on which they feed.

They are not blind and being highly skilled navigators are unlikely to be entangled in anyone's hair!

If your garden is large, and especially if it is in a rural area, you may succeed in attracting bats to it for summer roosting, particularly if you invest in a bat box as natural roosting sites become more scarce.

Roosts are needed for different reasons: in Summer, for use as a nesting roost and in Winter, for hibernation.

Bats are highly sensitive to chemicals so do **not** use timber preservatives.

Contact your local Bat Conservation Society. They will advise you on fixing bat boxes and the law, as bats are now a protected species and need all the help they can get.

bat ears!

Do *you* like mosquitoes? Bats love them!

BUMBLE-BEES

Both bumble-bees and honey-bees are major pollinators of fruit and flowers.

Sadly, the use of weed killers has reduced their food supply and intensive farming has resulted in the loss of rough grasslands and typical nesting sites, such as hedges.

With their own inbuilt, specialist central heating systems, and hairy bodies (for insulation), both bumble-bees and honey-bees can fly in much colder weather than many other insects.

Early Spring sees the young queen bumble-bee emerge from hibernation, to look for food and a possible nesting site. Watch as they fly just above the ground inspecting grass tussocks and holes in hedge banks or amongst dead vegetation.

Some nest above ground and others nest in old mouseholes. You may be able to tempt a queen to nest by providing a nesting site. Old compost heaps, mounds of leaf mould and log/brash piles have all been used.

You can make a nest by using an old upturned flower pot at least 23 cms in diameter. Partially fill it with old mouse nesting material and bury it in the ground. Insert a piece of hosepipe to act as the entrance, or cover the entrance hole with a piece of slate mounted on four small stones. This acts as a roof and keeps the weather out.

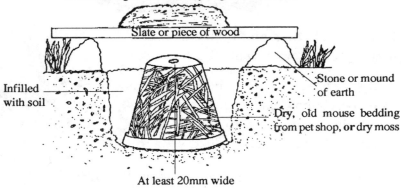

Stone, brick or sand to weigh wood down and keep it from being knocked off by dogs, children, etc.

Slate or piece of wood

Infilled with soil

Stone or mound of earth

Dry, old mouse bedding from pet shop, or dry moss

At least 20mm wide

Once a suitable site has been found the queen collects a cache of pollen, makes wax pots for storing honey to eat on cold, rainy days, and lays a few eggs.

She nurses, feeds, protects and incubates the young, which grow and each one makes a cocoon in which to pupate. These are the workers, which will then take over the running and building of the nest, leaving the queen to produce eggs. When Autumn comes they will all die, except for a few young queens who will mate and hibernate.

By planting from the following list we can help bumble-bees more:

Flowers: buttercup, Canterbury bells, clover, columbine, cornflower, cranesbill family, dahlia, devil's bit and field scabious, forget-me-not, foxglove, globe thistle, hemp agrimony, honesty, knapweed, lady's smock, limanthes douglasii, Michaelmas daisy, nasturtium, nigella (love-in-a-mist), phacelia tanacetifolia, poppy, purple loosestrife, sedum spectabile, sweet rocket, teasel, toad flax, viper's bugloss, wallflower, white dead nettle.

Herbs: borage, chives, clover, comfrey, hyssop, lavender, marjoram, mint family, rosemary, thyme.

Shrubs: buddleia, cotoneaster, flowering currant, hawthorn, honeysuckle, mahonia japonica.

Trees: fruit trees, pussy willow.

THE DREADED WASP!

During the summer months common wasps must be one of the most beneficial garden pest predators of all. They hunt for caterpillars, flies and other pests as well as patrolling plants and flower heads waiting for flies, which they pounce on, cut off their wings, decapitate, then carry off to their nests.

This 'meat' is then chewed up and softened by worker wasps, who feed it to the larvae. The adults feed on nectar and other sweet sugary foods but they lack the long tongues with which bees and butterflies are equipped.

After waking from hibernation, the fertilised queen will feed and look for a nest site. She constructs a nest by scraping off thin pieces of wood with her jaws, which she chews and mixes with saliva to form a paperlike pulp. After making a few cells she lays her eggs, starts to build an outer wall, then adds more cells.

This continues until the first eggs hatch. She feeds the grubs on small insects until they are big enough to carry on all of the queen's duties except for egg laying.

When Autumn arrives all wasps die except the fertilised queens.

It is the workers which are a pest around the picnic table — usually in late Summer or early Autumn. By then they are redundant and, with no young to care for, know their time is almost up. So they have a last binge before they die — and who can blame them!

HOVERFLIES

These are often mistaken for wasps and killed. Although mimicking a wasp a hoverfly is completely harmless, feeding on nectar and pollen as an adult and on greenfly as a larva. It actually does hover and lacks the long antennae found on wasps.

Its larva is blind and maggot-like, and found wherever there are greenfly. It crawls along plant stems towards the light and young growing tips, where its prey, the aphids, can be found. These, it consumes by the dozen prior to emerging as an adult.

Hoverflies need simple, flat, open flowers, to provide them with nectar for energy and pollen for their egg laying.

Plants liked by hoverflies:

Flowers: aster, baby blue eyes, buckwheat, buttercup, candytuft, coleus, convolvulus tricolor, limnanthes douglasii, nemophilia, phacelia tanacetifolia, rudbeckia, sedum spectabile, solidigo, yarrow.

Herbs: angelica, dill, fennel, horehound, hyssop, mustard, sweet cicely.

Trees: elder, rowan.

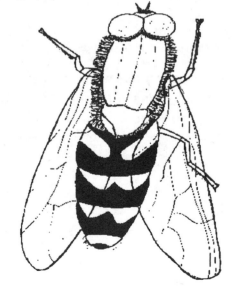

The completely harmless garden friend — the hoverfly. Unlike the wasp it has no long feelers (antennae).

LACEWINGS

Their transparent, lace-like wings, with an elaborate veined pattern, are much longer than their bodies. They also have very long antennae and large golden eyes. The green species is most often seen when the adults hibernate, sometimes in houses. They are then a pinkish colour as they produce their own antifreeze.

The six-legged larvae are voracious hunters of aphids, leafhoppers, scale insects and other soft-bodied pests, picking their prey up, raising it into the air, piercing it and sucking it dry. They then discard the dead skins, sometimes putting them onto their backs to act as camouflage from birds.

The adults find a colony of aphids and lay an egg on a single, thin stalk, which is left sticky as a deterrent. Their eggs can also sometimes be found in clumps on the underside of plant leaves.

Many die during the Winter because they have chosen a poor site in which to hibernate. Take a wooden box, the size of a bird's nesting box, stuff it with **dry** straw and make a few small entrance slits 1.5 cms wide on its underside. No entrance hole is needed.

Place it on a pole 1.5 metres high, in the open and away from trees and buildings, between August and November. Then put both box and contents inside a shed, placing it outside again in late February or early March, when the lacewings will emerge.

A 'lacewing hotel' can also be purchased for this purpose. (See Appendix for stockist.)

the ferocious, bristled larva

the adult's long and beautiful, lacy wings

LADYBIRDS

Both adults and larvae eat aphids and should always be welcome in our gardens.

There are no particular plants that can encourage them, although the nettle aphid breeds on nettles very early in Spring and the ladybird usually feasts on them, after waking from hibernation.

The larvae actually look very ugly and vicious. They have six legs and are usually slate blue/grey in colour, with white or orange spots down their body length. The bright yellow eggs (similar to those of the large cabbage white butterfly) are laid in clusters, usually, but not always, near aphid colonies.

The adults hibernate in dying or dead vegetation, behind tree bark, in leaf litter and hollow plant stems. Try to leave places for them to hibernate. Sometimes many hibernate together in favoured sites which are used year after year.

How these sites are found is not yet understood, although it has been suggested that they use pheromones or scents. The more ladybirds present, the more scent is produced, thereby enabling the scent to linger on for the next generation to find.

 The use of chemicals may not only kill ladybirds, their larvae and prey, but may affect the chemical scent left behind by the hibernating generation, thus making a favoured and successful hibernation site undiscovered by the next generation.

HARVESTMEN

These look like spiders with very long legs walking as if on stilts. They have no venom and do not produce webs like spiders, but hunt using their second pair of legs as feelers and usually stumble across their prey by climbing plant stems, walls or fences at night.

They need undisturbed areas of long grass, vegetation, compost heaps and leaf litter under hedges and trees.

Their head and thorax have fused into one body part, unlike spiders with their distinctive, separate sections, and they only have two eyes.

Having extremely long legs and walking above the ground has its advantages, as the first part to be grabbed is sure to be one of its legs! The harvestman can then detach this leg and the predator is only left with a leg whilst the original owner legs it!

It preys on small caterpillars, aphids and anything it can overpower.

DEVIL'S COACH-HORSE

This fierce looking beetle, with its matt, black colour and slender body about 3 cms long, adopts a scorpion-like posture when threatened, snapping its savage jaws in a threatening and aggressive manner.

It is a carnivore and scavenger, hunting at night and hiding from predators during the day. It eats all it can overpower, tackling large prey such as slugs and the distasteful cabbage white caterpillar.

It hides under stones, logs and leaf litter, in compost heaps and dead vegetation, and needs undisturbed areas with good ground cover.

CENTIPEDES

Because they are fast runners and rather creepy looking, many will have been crushed underfoot by people ignorant of the fact that this is a garden ally to be encouraged.

a flexible friend!

It is a hunter at night. A predator of slugs, worms, mites and small insects, it uses its powerful front jaws to seize and bite its prey, then inject it with poison.

Centipedes are long and thin, varying in colour according to their species, from chestnut brown to an orange/yellow. They all have segmented bodies, with one pair of legs per segment.

Centipedes live under stones and logs, amongst leaf litter, in compost heaps and sometimes in air spaces in the soil, using their long, thin, flexible bodies to snake in between soil particles.

They hunt in areas of undisturbed vegetation and need damp, dark places to hide from the sun, which can soon dry out and kill them.

GROUND BEETLES

These require similar living conditions to the devil's coach horse and are another voracious night-time predator.

Although it cannot fly, its shiny, black body, about 2.5 cms long, has much longer wing covers than the devil's coach horse. It also has a more distinct head, thorax and abdomen.

Experiments are underway to try and breed these beetles to use as a biological control for slugs. They relish the larva of the cabbage root fly but unfortunately they themselves are relished by hedgehogs!

Part Four

TREES

WHY PLANT TREES?

Trees, like hedges, are steeped in history, mythology, fertility rites, superstition, religion and, of course, have numerous practical uses.

Trees joined heaven and earth. The branches reached out to the spirits in the sky. The trunk, which could be touched, was in the real world — the present. The roots penetrated the underworld — the unknown.

The Green Man and the symbolism of life was represented in the branches of trees.

The ancient folk custom of tree dressing spans many cultures.

Objects such as rags and jewellery used to be attached to significant trees as an offering against ills and to promote good fortune.

'Touch wood' is a well known saying, supposed to bring good luck.

Yew was the wood used for the famous longbow and today its clippings are used to produce taxol, an alkaloid used in the treatment of certain cancers.

The oak tree supplied timber to build the naval ships, which brought wealth to Britain and its Empire.

The management of woodlands was of prime importance to our ancestors, who understood the importance of coppicing and pollarding trees, generating new life within the tree and creating new habitats which were quickly colonised by wildlife.

A thing of beauty is a joy forever.
Keats

CREATING A WOODLAND EDGE

For most gardens creating a wood or small copse would be impossible. However a woodland edge may well be a feasible option. Use native trees and shrubs as the backbone of the woodland edge, creating a rich and diverse woodland habitat.

Try to create different layers of vegetation in a tiered fashion — trees, shrubs, tall plants, smaller plants, ground level plants, a rich layer of leaf litter, dead logs, twigs and branches.

This gives wildlife the widest scope to colonise and live. Indeed, many species prefer their own tier in which to live, breed and forage for food.

The cycle of growth, death and decay in a woodland builds up a layer of rich organic matter, which is added to each year by trees bringing up nutrients from the soil and returning them again when the leaves fall.

You may gather leaf mould, or make it yourself from your own trees, to create this important part of the woodland edge. Leaf mould is an important habitat for numerous species of insects and plants. Sycamore leaf mould is not as good as oak or beech.

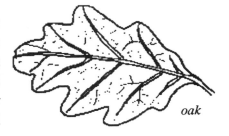

oak

Incorporate leaf mould into the soil when planting, then use it as a mulch round the newly-planted trees and shrubs. Shredded or chopped forest bark is a good substitute available from garden centres.

PLANTING A BARE-ROOTED TREE

Before planting ...

Consider how to avoid possible root damage to flags, drains, walls, foundations, fences and lawns, which might cause subsidence.

Consider the proximity to buildings. What light and shade will the branches cast?

Many of the principles used when planting hedges apply also to trees.

The choice of species is paramount — the tree's height, spread and its correct situation must be carefully considered.

Keep the roots of bare-rooted trees **moist at all times** before planting, and sheltered from the wind.

Lightly firm soil around roots both during and after planting.

A cross bar stake about a third of the way up the trunk allows the tree to move in the wind. This rocking movement has been found to thicken the trunk and the tree grows more anchorage roots.

Use tree tie or old rubber cycle inner tube.

Optional piping. Insert funnel and pour water in.

Cover soil with black plastic after a mulch of organic matter.

Retaining wall of soil assists watering of root system.

Insert fork and lightly loosen side walls.

Break up sub-soil and add organic matter.

Planting a Tree

Ensure all perennial and annual weeds and grasses are removed. Grass is more efficient than a tree at stealing water, with more fibrous roots and less greenery above ground from which water can transpire.

Lack of water stops root growth and the tree closes its stomata (the pores in the epidermis — the thin outer layer of cells which cover the leaves). These allow carbon dioxide to enter the leaves for photosynthesis, and water loss (transpiration) to occur. When inhibited the tree's growth slows down, stops, and eventually the tree dies.

Compaction has its effect on roots. If a trench is dug in a compacted area roots grow till they reach compaction, then turn and grow inwards. Loosen the soil in the trench sides, using a fork.

Water is vital to any tree and, as with hedges, a mulch can mean life or death for it. Build a small wall of earth around the tree, into which water can be poured and thus directed straight to the roots.

Trees grow much better with weed and grass control, even with a nitrogen fertiliser, which can encourage vigorous grass growth.

Strimmers and mowers can damage tree trunks. Use a strimmer guard or plant the tree in a growing tube.

Woodlands are usually damp places with moisture held in leaf mould. Position your woodland edge so that it avoids the midday sun, or the leaf mould may dry out and limit the plants you can use.

If tempted to plant a larger, older tree for an instant effect, remember that young trees establish faster than older ones and are less expensive.

Large trees may need staking.

Planting whips about two metres apart will quickly establish a woodland edge and later can be selectively thinned out or coppiced.

Allow trees two years to get established prior to underplanting with wildflowers, which will compete for water. Then plant established plant plugs as opposed to scattering woodland seed mixtures, most of which will not survive.

PLANTING FROM SEED

Most people obtain their trees as bare rooted or pot grown plants. There are millions of tree seeds made available every Autumn which just go to waste. There is no more mystique in planting tree seeds than in growing flowers or vegetables from seed.

Thousands of people have been involved in a massive initiative called 'Seeds of Time and Place'. (See Appendix for contact details.) Local people and school children collect local tree seeds and plant them locally, thus ensuring that their local woodlands and hedgerows are regenerated and that the local bio-diversity is not diluted with foreign species.

Some people have collected and planted seeds from trees which hold a special memory for them. It is alright to collect seeds from the ground but is illegal to trespass to collect them. Ask permission first.

 Seeds, such as acorns and beech mast, can be collected in Autumn. Using a hessian or an onion bag will let the seeds breathe and the addition of leaf mould will prevent them from drying out.

Plastic carrier bags cause sweating. Seeds which do not have a fruit covering may rot or go mouldy. They can also heat up and dry out if kept in sunlight for even a short time.

Plant acorns very quickly, as once dried out they may not germinate.

As with wild flowers, some tree seeds need at least one period, and some need more, of cold. This process is called stratification. It is provided naturally by wintry conditions. Most seeds will have been 'sown' in the wild before the Winter and covered with dead leaves, which rot down to produce leaf mould.

Seeds which are surrounded by fruit, such as hawthorn or crab apple, **can** be collected and stored in polythene bags, as it is only the flesh which rots or goes mouldy; the seeds inside remain moist.

If you are unable to sow the seeds soon after collection, or start any treatment such as stratification, store them in a cool, dark place away from rodents. **A fridge is ideal for all seeds.**

Seeds such as hawthorn are covered in flesh which contains a chemical growth inhibitor. This is nature's way of protecting the seed and ensuring it does not germinate at the wrong time of year. This inhibitor has to be completely removed for growth to start.

There are two ways to achieve this. One is to ask a friendly blackbird to eat the berry and deposit it a day or so later into your prepared plant pot or 'rootrainer'!

The other way is to physically remove all the flesh yourself, by immersing it in warm water, squeezing the flesh and scrubbing it off with a scrubbing brush. The flesh and skin floats around in the water so scoop off this pulp. The seeds themselves sink. (If they float do not use them.) Pour all the water away, then store your seeds until sowing time. This immersion test can be done with many tree seeds.

Acorns or hazelnuts are sometimes eaten by grubs from inside the shell. Put them into water to see if they float or sink. Discard the ones which float.

Tall oaks from little acorns grow.

'ROOTRAINERS'

An excellent success rate can be obtained when growing trees from seed by using a 'rootrainer'. These are premoulded plastic cells that come hinged together like two pages of an open book, with four cells per page. Trays are available with eight pages — 32 trees.

The cells can be closed together and locked into position. The folding action causes the hinge to split open, allowing air to circulate at the bottom of the cell and water to be soaked up. The shape and design of the cells trains the growing roots downwards and the cells can be opened in order to observe the roots without disturbing them..

Choose a suitable peat-free compost. Coir, with its superior water retaining properties and loose friable structure, is an ideal medium for growing trees.

Immersion in a weak solution of liquid seaweed may help the seeds to germinate. Using this solution to moisten the growing medium may also enhance their chance of germination.

Insert all the 'closed' pages into the holder and fill up with the seaweed moistened growing medium. If you are going away for several weeks and will be unable to water your trees, it may be a good idea to mix in some water retaining granules at this stage. Some commercial growers also add slow release fertiliser, such as Osmocote.

Fill the individual cells and gently tap down the holder to settle the compost. Do **not** use your fingers to firm the compost down as an open structure will encourage root growth.

Larger seeds need burying. Smaller seeds, such as birch, can be sown on top of the compost and lightly covered with vermiculite. Overwinter them outside for stratification. As with flowers, label the seeds, then cover with netting to foil both birds and vermin.

silver birch

As Spring approaches cover the pages and container with a clear plastic tray to encourage germination. If none germinate your seed may need another cold period. This could mean another Winter or a deal struck with your partner to place them in the fridge for a few weeks. Unlikely but worth a try!

If the seeds do germinate, remove the propagation lid and keep an eye on their water needs. Water by immersing both container and pages.

Use a weak solution of seaweed extract mixed with the water. This is a critical period in a young tree's life and this feeding could mean the difference between success or failure.

Liquid seaweed encourages a strong, healthy root system and offers some protection against certain diseases. It is of special benefit to fruit trees and can also be safely sprayed onto leaves as a foliar feed.

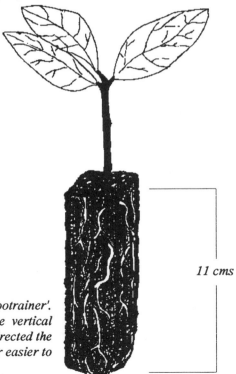

11 cms

Young tree grown from seed in 'rootrainer'. Notice its good root system — the vertical grooves of the 'rootrainer' having directed the roots downwards. Such trees are far easier to plant than bare-rooted specimens.

Once roots emerge from the base of the cells you need to raise the container and cells off the ground, 3 to 4 cms will do. Otherwise the roots will continue to grow, wrapping and entwining around each other in the shade of the neighbouring cells, seeking water.

This lifting creates an air gap and stops the main root from growing. It is known as air pruning. The tree then grows finer roots within the cell, giving a more fibrous root system — ideal for any young plant prior to being planted out in its final planting position.

Once Autumn has come insert stakes if needed, dig a hole and plant out your tree seedlings. Firm the soil round the roots at the sides and on top. Attach your growing tube, water in and wait for Spring.

Don't throw away your washing-up water, use it to water your trees. However, as any detergent will kill some of the natural bacteria which breaks down organic matter to release minerals for the growing tree, this water should not be used more than once a fortnight. So rotate which trees are watered with it.

Consider buying native trees grown from seed. (See Appendix for stockist.)

TREE GROWING — KITS AND CUTTINGS

 **Tree growing kits** are available and contain coconut coir bricks, 'rootrainers', a plastic holder, propagation lid, tree seeds, slow release fertiliser and water retaining crystals — in fact, everything you need to 'Sow and Grow a Wood on a Windowsill'. (See Appendix for stockists.)

Be wary of planting horse chestnut and sycamore seeds — sometimes called 'weed trees'. Although easily grown they out-shade, and out-compete with, other trees. Native trees are far better for wildlife.

Growing trees from cuttings is another cheap and cheerful idea. Willows are easily grown using this method. Willow 'withies' can be used to grow a 'fedge' — a living fence and hedge. This can be woven into many different shapes and sculptures, or even into a living seat!

In Autumn, after all growth has stopped, cut young (this year's) wood from your chosen willow, removing all leaves. You are looking for straight lengths, about 30 cms long and the thickness of a pencil.

Although not absolutely necessary you can prepare your 'withy' nursery beforehand by digging moisture-retaining organic matter into the soil. Cover this area with black plastic.

Insert a long metal pole into the soil through the black plastic, to a depth of about 23 cms. Then plant the cutting into the hole. You can plant all your cuttings as close as 7.5 cms apart. The black plastic will greatly enhance the success of the cuttings by suppressing weed growth and retaining moisture.

By early Spring the cuttings which have taken will show signs of growth, with sprouting leaves. Keep them watered and left in place until the end of the growing season, then gently dig up your new, young trees, complete with new root systems, and plant them up.

bluebell
bugle
daffodil (wild)
foxglove
garlic mustard

bluebell

grape hyacinth
hedgerow cranesbill
hedge woundwort
nettle-leaved bell flower
primrose
red campion
St John's wort (perforated)
stitchwort (lesser and greater)
sweet violet
white dead nettle (can be rampant)

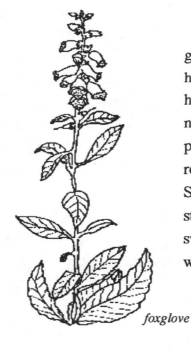

foxglove

wild garlic
wild strawberry
wood cranesbill
wood forget-me-not
yellow archangel

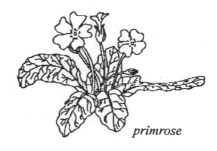

primrose

TREES FOR GARDENS AND WILDLIFE

Species	Growth	Insects	Fruit	Seed	Coppice	Hedge
Alder	Average	Few	-	Yes	Yes	-

Comments: Nitrogen fixer. Damp places. Siskins and goldfinches.

Bird Cherry	Average	Few	Yes	-	-	-

Comments: Bitter berries loved by birds.

Crab Apple	Average	Yes	Yes	-	-	-

Comments: Pollinator of many cultivated apples. John Downie recommended.

Downy Birch	Fast	Yes	-	Yes	Yes	-

Comments: Can grow on damper soil than silver birch. Good for caterpillars.

Hawthorn	Fast	Yes	Yes	-	Yes	Yes

Comments: Excellent for nectar and berries.

Hazel	Slow	Few	-	Nuts	Yes	Yes

Comments: Early catkins. Nuts for mammals and birds.

Holly	Slow	Few	Yes	-	Yes	Yes

Comments: Prickly evergreen. Holly blue butterfly. Berries on wild female only.

Oak	Slow	Yes	-	Yes	Yes	Yes

Comments: The most useful tree of all. Grow saplings and prune to size.

Osier	Very Fast	Yes	-	-	Yes	-

Comments: Early nectar/pollen. Good for caterpillars. Useful branches (withies). The osier, Salix Viminalis, is easy to grow from a cutting.

Species	Growth	Insects	Fruit	Seed	Coppice	Hedge
Pussy Willow	Very Fast	Yes	-	-	Yes	-

Comments: Damp places. Good for insects. Early nectar/pollen for bees.

Species	Growth	Insects	Fruit	Seed	Coppice	Hedge
Rowan	Average	Few	Yes	-	-	-

Comments: Casts only light shade. Early berries.

Species	Growth	Insects	Fruit	Seed	Coppice	Hedge
Silver Birch	Fast	Yes	-	Yes	Yes	-

Comments: Colonising tree. Drier conditions than downy birch. Good for insects.

Species	Growth	Insects	Fruit	Seed	Coppice	Hedge
Spindle	Very Fast	Few	Yes	-	-	-

Comments: Unusual pinkish berries. Red leaves in Autumn.

Species	Growth	Insects	Fruit	Seed	Coppice	Hedge
Wayfaring	Average	Few	Yes	-	-	-

Comments: Red berries turn black. Large flowerhead with many white flowers.

Species	Growth	Insects	Fruit	Seed	Coppice	Hedge
Whitbeam	Average	Few	Yes	-	-	-

Comments: Used as decorative street tree. Excellent for berries.

Species	Growth	Insects	Fruit	Seed	Coppice	Hedge
Yew	Slow	Few	Yes	-	-	Yes

Comments: Scarlet berries contrast with dark evergreen needles. Good shelter.

Scots pine

There are numerous reference books available to check on the eventual height of your trees. Some can be coppiced (cut back to near ground level). Most tree species will grow reasonably well on most types of soil. Check with your local nurseryman.

Part Five

HEDGES

THE HISTORY OF HEDGES

For centuries man and hedge co-existed together. Hedges are a man-made feature, quickly colonised by wildflowers and wildlife.

Hedgehog, hedge sparrow and hedge woundwort are reminders of this past association.

The Anglo Saxon Chronicles mention King Ida of Northumberland making a hedge at the fortified Bamburgh.

During the time of the Black Death hedges were plundered for their herbal remedies and charms to ward off evil spirits. Yet, with fewer people to tend them, many became overgrown. People died while hedges thrived.

The Enclosures Act changed the face of the countryside. A vaste number of hedgerows were planted on rough pastureland and common land to make small fields.

This caused many conflicts between the commoners and the new owners of these fields. Their rights were being eroded. Laws were made to protect hedges and punish those who damaged them.

At one time hedges were much more important to man than they are today. They were an economic resource and as such they were managed and tended.

History, folklore and traditions, unless of economic value, have no place in today's society and thousands of miles of hedgerow have been grubbed out and lost forever, along with the importance they once held for mankind and wildlife.

Hopefully, this is now being redressed and the new hedgerow regulations of 1997 **may** go some **small** way towards this.

THE USE OF HEDGES

Hedges provided man with food, fuel, medicines, windbreaks, fodder, timber, barriers, defence of homesteads, boundaries, protection and drinks, as well as becoming a part of folklore.

Cattle could be penned in, protected from predators, given shelter from rain, wind and sun, and fed both from the hedge itself and from the plants around it.

Food for both animals and man was provided from a hedge's leaves, roots, stems, fruit and nuts.

Plants growing under a hedge also provided food. Some of these were chickweed, mushrooms, nettles, cleavers, garlic, sow thistle and blackberries.

Fancy a drink? Make one using elder flowers, yarrow leaves or rose hips. Something a little stronger? Try nettle wine, nettle beer or birch sap wine.

Tansy, garlic mustard, cow parsley and lady's smock were used as flavourings in food.

Dyes of many different colours were obtained from the leaves, stems, roots, bark, nuts, seeds, flowers and mosses found in hedgerows.

A rough cloth was made from the tough, fibrous stems of nettles.

Light timber from the hedge was used for making rakes, handles, oars, arrow shafts, brooms, hurdles, portable cattle and sheep pens, wattle for walls, stakes, fuel and charcoal.

Specimen trees, such as oak, ash and elm, when allowed to grow on, provided heavy timber for a house builder's planks, beams and roofs.

Medicines and herbal remedies were made. Oils, balms, poultices, ointments and drinks were concocted, to heal the body and drive away evil spirits attacking the mind. Eyebright, lungwort, stitchwort, woundwort and selfheal had specific curing abilities, as their names suggest.

A hedge today is used either to mark a boundary or to act as a decorative feature.

Dependency on hedges has almost disappeared, along with many of its old uses. However, hedges are becoming an increasingly important habitat for our beleaguered flowers and animals.

Nesting, shelter, hibernation sites, song posts, territorial boundaries, safe havens, food, cover, wildlife corridors linking one habitat to another, and breeding sites, are a few of the assets a hedgerow provides for wildlife.

Visit your local Hedgerow supermarket!

A Shopping List

Porridge	Tools
Dye	Nuts
Soup	Mushrooms
Medicine	Fuel
Beer	Fodder
Wine	Timber
Herbs	Air Freshener
Syrup	Oils
Balms	Cloth
Fruit	Food

THE CASE FOR USING NATIVE PLANTS

Why use native wildflower seeds, trees and hedging plants?

Wildlife and plants have evolved together during thousands of years. They co-exist together in a successful, stable habitat.

More and more people are planting wildflowers, trees and hedgerows to help our wildlife and to enhance their own local environment.

Many of the hedgerow species planted, especially hawthorn, have been imported from eastern Europe and sold in British garden centres and nurseries.

Stock, especially seeds from eastern Europe where seed sorting technology is not as advanced as ours, may well contain species which grow more aggressively than our own and quickly swamp the indigenous species.

Labour costs are cheaper in eastern European countries and it is questionable whether the species imported from there have been grown in nurseries or uprooted from the wild, thereby depleting their own native stock.

Insisting on British grown stock will raise the awareness of our own nurserymen and encourage them to grow native species. This may well benefit local jobs.

Planting British grown stock ensures that the genetic biodiversity is not diluted by cross fertilising with foreign stock.

The buds, flowers and fruits of non-native hawthorn develop at slightly different times than our native species. They are also more susceptible to mildew.

This growth rate differential may well impede and retard the growth rate of caterpillars feeding on the leaves, thus leaving them open to predators and parasites for a longer period.

When planting an area, notice what is already growing successfully there, taking into account the local climate, the soil condition and the habitat in which you wish to plant. Think local first, then national.

Local parks and nature reserves often weed out young native trees and hedgerow plants. Ask permission to take them home to plant if you live locally.

Try growing trees from locally gathered seeds or berries. Patience is needed! With hawthorn, scrub off the flesh completely as it contains a germination inhibiting chemical, then chip the hard outer seed coat to soften it up prior to germination.

Stock obtained from abroad can harbour alien pests and diseases. The New Zealand flat worm immediately springs to mind. Buying British lessens this danger.

Buddleia is an exception. Although not native no such species exists here and it enhances our own nectar-producing shrubs and plants.

Wild flowers growing either side of a hedgerow — a rare sight today.

HEDGES FOR WILDLIFE

Species	Growth	Insects	Fruit	Seed	Mixed Hedge
Barberry	Average	Yes	Yes	-	Yes

Comments: Thorny. Many cultivated species.

Species	Growth	Insects	Fruit	Seed	Mixed Hedge
Beech	Slow	Few	-	Mast	Yes

Comments: Keeps leaves in Winter. Good cover. May not produce mast as hedge.

Species	Growth	Insects	Fruit	Seed	Mixed Hedge
Blackthorn	Fast	Yes	Yes	-	Yes

*Comments: Very early flowers. Nectar. Sloes. **Suckers** sent out along the ground.*

Species	Growth	Insects	Fruit	Seed	Mixed Hedge
Buckthorn	Average	Yes	Yes	-	Yes

Comments: Food plant for brimstone butterfly caterpillars.

Species	Growth	Insects	Fruit	Seed	Mixed Hedge
Cotoneaster	Average	Yes	Yes	-	Yes

Comments: Excellent for bumble bees and honey bees. Many species. Some grow against the wall.

Species	Growth	Insects	Fruit	Seed	Mixed Hedge
Goat (Pussy) Willow	Very Fast	Very Good	-	-	Yes

Comments: Open growth. Good for moths/caterpillars, nectar/pollen, small birds. Cultivated species available.

Species	Growth	Insects	Fruit	Seed	Mixed Hedge
Guelder Rose	Moderate	Yes	Yes	-	Yes

Comments: Early flowers. Nectar/pollen for hoverflies and other insects.

Species	Growth	Insects	Fruit	Seed	Mixed Hedge
Hazel	Slow	Yes	-	Nuts	Yes

Comments: Good coppicing. Early catkins. Nectar/pollen.

Species	Growth	Insects	Fruit	Seed	Mixed Hedge
Hawthorn	Fast	Very Good	Very Good	-	Yes

Comments: Thorny. Dense if pruned/layered. Good nectar/pollen. Excellent hedge.

Species	Growth	Insects	Fruit	Seed	Mixed Hedge
Holly	Slow	Yes	Yes	-	Yes

Comments: Food plant for holly blue butterfly caterpillars. Good cover. Evergreen. Only the female wild holly produces berries.

Species	Growth	Insects	Fruit	Seed	Mixed Hedge
Hornbeam	Slow	Few	-	Keys	Yes

Comments: Keeps leaves in Winter. Good cover. Can grow in clay soils.

Species	Growth	Insects	Fruit	Seed	Mixed Hedge
Lavender	Moderate	Yes	-	Yes	No

Comments: Best as single species hedge. Butterflies and bees love it. Goldfinches enjoy the seeds.

Species	Growth	Insects	Fruit	Seed	Mixed Hedge
Oak	Slow	Very good	-	Acorns	Yes

Comments: Can be grown with mixed hedge and pruned to hedge shape.

Species	Growth	Insects	Fruit	Seed	Mixed Hedge
Privet (wild)	Fast	Yes	Yes	-	Yes

Comments: Good nectar. Butterflies. Slightly thorny. Privet hawkmoth.

Species	Growth	Insects	Fruit	Seed	Mixed Hedge
Pyracantha	Moderate	Yes	Yes	-	Yes

Comments: Thorny. Good against a wall or fence.

Species	Growth	Insects	Fruit	Seed	Mixed Hedge
Rosa Rugosa	Fast	Yes	Yes	Yes	Yes

Comments: Greenfinches find seeds in large hips. Thorny.

Species	Growth	Insects	Fruit	Seed	Mixed Hedge
Skimmia Japonica	Moderate	Yes	Yes	-	Yes

Comments: Decorative. Many cultivated species.

Species	Growth	Insects	Fruit	Seed	Mixed Hedge
Spindle	Very fast	Yes	Yes	-	Yes

Comments: Good nectar. Unusual berries.

Species	Growth	Insects	Fruit	Seed	Mixed Hedge
Yew	Very Slow	Few	Yes	-	Yes

Comments: Evergreen and dense. Poisonous seed within berry.

PLANTING A HEDGE

By planting a hedge not only will you be providing for your local wildlife but you will also be continuing the historical link mankind has had with hedges.

However, hedges do take time to become established — anything from three to four years or more. They are not really practical in a small garden. Consider climbers.

A hedge needs managing and tending. Each shrub is an individual tree and if allowed to grow on will become a mature, tall, leggy tree.

You can see remnants of old hedges in the open countryside, planted in line, left unmanaged and now dying, having become old trees.

Most single species hedgerows have limited value for wildlife, for example conifers. These may offer a nesting site, winter cover and some insects for food. However, hawthorn is much better.

A mixed, native hedge offers a variety of leaves for insects, which in turn means more food for birds. Flowers, nuts and fruit provide food for insects, birds and mammals.

Different hedge species come into leaf, flower and fruit at different times throughout the year, thereby extending the possible food availability to wildlife.

The more diverse is the habitat next to an established hedge, for example trees, wild flowers, grasses, ditches, marshes, the more species of wildlife will be found there.

Plant hedges to form a corridor linking one side of the garden to the other. Wrens, in particular, feel vulnerable when flying across an open lawn.

Plant a hedge in front of a wooden fence. Better still, **replace** it with a hedge!

Hedges do not have to be planted in straight lines. Consider a gentle 'S' shape or even a curved hedge. It creates a more diverse micro-habitat for wildlife.

A hedge can offer a refuge for woodland, shade-loving plants on one side and sun-loving, field boundary plants on the other.

SHAPES OF LINEAR HEDGES

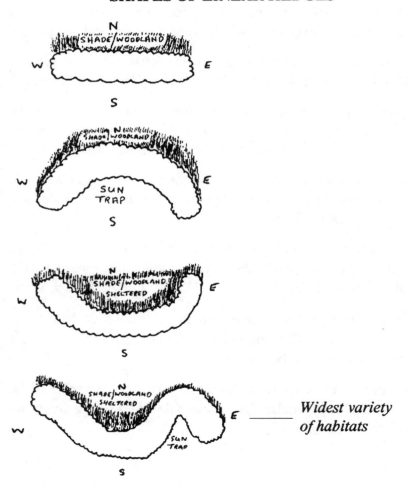

Widest variety of habitats

TIPS FOR PLANTING HEDGES

What you need: Canes or sticks, string, spade, fork, organic matter, bonemeal (optional), hedging plants, weed suppressing material or mulch, protective tree tubes (optional).

Bare rooted, two-year-old whips are much cheaper than pot grown plants. Ensure that they have an extensive root system.

Heel whips into moist soil if not ready to plant and **always** ensure roots are kept moist at **all** times.

When planting keep the roots covered either by a moist cloth or soil and keep this in a plastic bag or a bucket of water.

For some whips as little as five minutes without protection from a drying wind or the hot sun is enough to kill them.

Plant between October and March. October and November are the best months as the soil is still warm, encouraging root growth.

For a single row hedge dig the trench 45 cms wide. Put the plants in 30 cms apart.

A double row hedge, with plants staggered, thickens the hedge and leaves no gaps if a few plants die. For this, dig a trench 75 cms wide. Allow 30 cms between rows and put the plants in 25 cms apart.

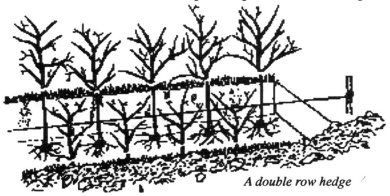

A double row hedge

Depending on the length of the hedge plant a native tree just outside the hedge — one which casts little shade, such as a birch or rowan.

A good mixture for a hedge would consist of three-quarters hawthorn, with the rest a mixture of blackthorn, holly, hazel and hornbeam.

Holly is shade tolerant and can be planted beside existing walls and fences, or on either side of a tree planted next to the hedge.

A STEP BY STEP GUIDE

Decide on the shape and length of hedge.
Is it to be a single or double row hedge?
Insert cane/stick at each end of hedge position. Tie string to each cane and tighten.

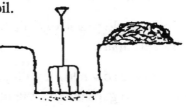

Remove a spade's depth of turf/soil for width of hedge planting area.

Use fork to break up compacted subsoil.
Insert to full length of prongs.
Push forward and back along full length of trench.
Start at one end and walk backwards.

Start at one end and stand on plank of wood.
Work backwards and add as much organic matter as possible.
Work it into the broken-down subsoil.
Add bonemeal, to help establish the roots.
Gently firm soil in trench bottom, to remove air pockets.

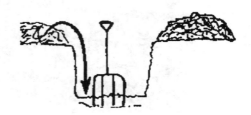

Look for soil mark and plant hedging plant at same depth.

The dotted line denotes the area where roots will collect water.

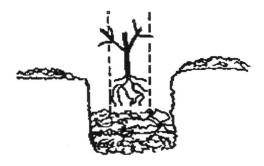

By spreading out the roots the widest possible water catchment area is achieved.

Tease out roots of container grown plants.

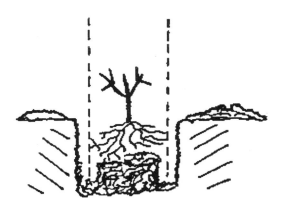

If the trench is in heavy clay or inhospitable soil, loosen the side walls with the fork prior to planting. This will allow the roots to penetrate and not encourage them to stay in the composted trench.

Replace soil and lightly firm around roots and stem. This ensures roots are in contact with soil and helps to anchor the plant.

Mulch area with organic matter or, if planting in grass, replace turf grass-side down along length of hedge.

Research has shown that the survival of hedges and trees is greatly enhanced if competition from weeds and grass is eliminated.

The root system of grass is extensive. It grows fast and is much more effective in taking up water than are young hedging plants and trees.

For best results, aim to keep a one metre diameter circle around the young plants free from grass and weeds for three years.

Although chemicals can be effective, aim to be organic and use alternative methods as described below ...

Permeable

Newspaper (several layers thick), cardboard, old carpet and various proprietory weed suppressing materials are effective. Cover them with grass, bark, wood chips or dead leaves for a natural effect.

An organic mulch 7.5 to 10 cms deep, of garden compost, well rotted manure or leaf mould, suppresses weeds, retains moisture, encourages beneficial soil life and builds soil fertility. This can be covered with wood chips or bark. Apply the mulch not later than May and water the ground beforehand, as rain may not penetrate to the roots.

Non-permeable

Black plastic makes an effective weed suppressing mulch and can be anchored by slotting it into the surrounding turf using a spade. Cover with wood chips or bark for a natural effect.

Do not plant any climbers, for instance honeysuckle, ivy or wild flowers, in your hedge for three years. The hedge will be well established then and able to compete effectively for water.

In the summer months a bucketful of water **per plant** once a week is more beneficial than using a hose pipe on the whole planted area.

Protective tree growing tubes (not rabbit spirals) create a favourable micro-climate, protect from rabbits and can easily be filled with water, which will soak in right above the roots.

A newly planted hedge, if cut down to 7.5 cms, will encourage side shoots and be bushier. Lay black plastic over the hedge. With a spade slot it into the soil on one side, pull tight and slot into the other side. Push the hedging plants through slits made in the black plastic and an instant mulch is achieved.

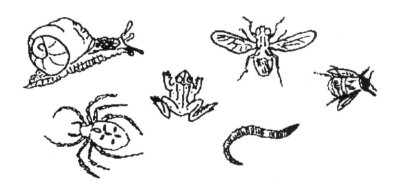

Numerous species inhabit and enrich our hedgerows.

HEDGE CUTTING

Points to consider:

Continually cutting hedges can deprive insects, birds and mammals of the flowers, fruit and berries which hedges produce. Many hedges produce their fruit on last year's growth.

Cutting hedges at the same height and width every year can result in the growing/sprouting tips becoming woody and tough, so losing their ability to produce new growth.

Cutting about 2 cms above last year's cut encourages a bushier, denser hedge and keeps the hedge full of vigour and growth.

A newly planted hawthorn hedge can be cut down to 7.5 cms. It seems brutal but encourages side shoots and makes a bushier hedge.

Hedges do need management. Left unmanaged the conservation value of a hedge is depleted, as some individual trees will grow on and shade out the habitat at the base of both the hedge and other trees.

Have you inherited a large, overgrown hawthorn hedge? Consider coppicing it in stages over a period of several years.

Adopt a varied cutting scheme. **Either** cut your hedges in a two or three year rotation, **or** cut just one or two sides, leaving the top for free growth. Then cut the top after two or three years.

Consider the Wildlife:

Cut at the end of January or in February, leaving the berries and nuts as a winter larder for birds and animals until then.

Birds like a variety of hedgerow height and density in which to nest. Try to cater for their needs.

Do not cut during the nesting season — March to August.

Hedgerow junctions offer escape routes for birds being chased by predators. Allow such junctions to grow freely.

Part Six

WILDFLOWERS

WHY GROW WILDFLOWERS?

As with hedges and trees, over the centuries countrymen have learnt many fascinating facts about wildflowers and found uses for them. Folklore tells us of their medicinal, nutritional and even magical properties. And don't mention woad to the Romans!

Many wild flower species have evolved and adapted to live in certain habitats, such as woodlands, marshes and hay meadows. Many of these habitats are diminishing at an alarming rate and many 'common' wildflowers are no longer common.

When a valued art treasure is sold abroad, or a famous building whether ancient or modern, is to be demolished, there is a public outcry. Some buildings are even graded and special permission needed before renovations can be carried out. Yet our wildflowers and meadows are disappearing rapidly and these are part of our history and heritage just as much, if not more so, than buildings.

Wildflowers also form part of our land's natural biodiversity and are a storehouse for genetic material which could well hold many secrets yet to be discovered, especially for use in the medicines of the future, or even as a potential food source.

Sadly, with many wildflowers in decline so is the wildlife which needs them to survive. The growing of wildflowers and certain garden plants can enhance our gardens both for ourselves and for the local wildlife. And as more wildflower plants and seeds become available, so we must all sow and grow wildflowers.

foxglove

WORDS AND THEIR MEANINGS

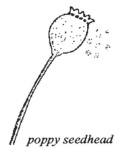

poppy seedhead

Annuals, for example the corn poppy, are grown from seed. They flower and die in the same season.

Biennials, for example the foxglove, are grown from seed and produce leaves and/or stems in the first season. They flower the following year, set seed and die.

Perennials, for example knapweed, are grown from seed, produce leaves and stems, then often flower and set seed in their first season. The foliage then dies down and new growth emerges the following year. These plants can be long lived.

Wildflower plugs are small, robust plants with strong, established root-balls, grown in modular plant trays.

Scarification Seeds which have a hard outer coat, for example the cranesbill and legume families, need to have this softened or weakened to allow moisture to penetrate and the germination process to start. To do this either rub the seed with sandpaper or nick it with a penknife.

Stratification These seeds need a period of cold prior to germination. Examples are the poppy, primrose, hemp agrimony, bramble, ragged robin and cowslip. Mix the seeds with damp sand and place them in the fridge for two months, to mimic the winter period. Do not put them in the freezer.

WILDFLOWER SEEDS

Wildflowers have evolved over countless years, each finding its own means of seed dispersal, either by ejection, falling to the ground or being eaten by birds or mammals. They may also be carried by the wind, on the fur of wild animals or even on our clothes.

Seeds have different periods before they germinate. Some germinate annually, others biennially, and some can remain dormant in the soil for many years.

Generally, if you wish to grow annual wildflowers then grow them from seed, which is far cheaper than buying wildflower plugs.

As many annuals resent any root disturbance, either sow them directly into their final flowering position, or sow them in small pots or 'propapacks'. These have individual cells, leaving the roots undisturbed when lifted. (See Appendix for stockist.)

For biennials and perennials consider using wildflower plugs.

The conditions for germination have differences as well. Some seeds need stratification or scarification, some germinate readily when fresh then go into dormancy as they dry, others germinate readily at almost any time of year.

Whatever you decide to buy, seeds or plants, purchase them from a reputable dealer and ask whether the seeds are of British origin.

Refer to the seed packet for precise sowing advice. Ensure the seeds are native to this country and **never** dig up wildflowers from the wild.

Although highly adaptable, wildflowers thrive best in conditions which imitate their natural habitat, whether it be marsh, meadow or woodland.

Simply scattering your expensive packet of wildflower seed mixture along your hedgerow or in woodland will be very disheartening and a waste of both time and money. Most will not germinate and, of those which do, many will not survive.

If you do sow wildflower seeds and they have not germinated, don't throw the seed tray or pots away in disgust. Have patience, some can take two or even three years to germinate.

Unlike plants like dandelion and chickweed, the seed of which readily germinates given the slightest opportunity, many wildflower seeds need a thorough preparation of the soil, which initially needs to be kept weed-free. The soil type and its condition will have a definite influence on successful germination and plant growth.

poppy

Buying wildflower seeds ...

Specialist wildflower seed companies offer wildflower seeds of plants suitable for particular areas, or attractive to specific wildlife, for example butterflies.

Such areas could include ponds or marshes, dry stone walls or rockeries, exposed or shady places, or others which are damp or dry or have acid or alkaline soil.

Reputable companies also supply the necessary, high quality, non-aggressive grass species with their wildflower meadow mixtures. By weight, they comprise about 20% wildflower seed to 80% grass seed.

The right mix can prove extremely important in the successful establishment and growth of the wildflowers.

PLUGS OR POT GROWN?

Many wildflowers are either biennial or perennial and as such are best grown in modules or pots, then planted out later into their final flowering position.

If you are planting a large number, buy modular grown plugs and pot them on yourself into 7.5 cm pots using a good compost. Plugs work out considerably cheaper than buying pot-grown wildflowers direct from a nursery or garden centre.

Well rooted wildflower plugs will, if planted correctly, establish, survive and prosper. The same cannot be said of wildflower seedlings or seeds. Plugs are more expensive but can give an almost instant result, leading to a spectacular display.

The best time to plant is the Autumn. The roots then grow and establish themselves in their new 'home' when the soil is still warm and moist. You want the roots to grow now, not waste the plant's energy, producing leaves and flowers.

Keep the plants in their trays or pots and dunk them in a bucket of water prior to planting, to ensure that they are thoroughly soaked. Also, soak the planting area both before and after planting.

Water is vital to the plant's establishment and, in Spring or Summer, may be needed every day if dry weather prevails. Watering should be thorough and not just a light sprinkling. If it does not penetrate deep into the soil the roots turn upwards to seek water and can be scorched as the sun dries the soil.

It is far quicker if planting a large number of plugs to place them all in their planting position prior to planting.

When planting make a hole with a trowel, or bulb planter, to the **required** depth. Plant the plug and firm the soil around it with the trowel, then lightly firm the soil on top with your feet.

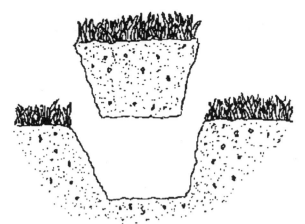

A plug of soil removed with a bulb planter, to plant
a pot grown wildflower into an existing lawn.

Leaving air gaps in the soil around the roots, and not firming in the plugs, can lead to failure. Test by gently tugging at a leaf. The plug should stay where it is if planted correctly, even if the leaf tears a little or snaps.

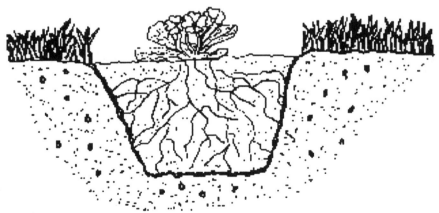

A well rooted, pot grown wildflower, perfectly planted.

Many perennial and biennial wildflowers are slow growers in their early stages and if grown from seed scattered in their final flowering position could well be hard to identify when weeding. They may also become shaded out by more vigorous annual weeds and grasses.

WHY PLANT A MEADOW?

The vast majority of people alive today will never have seen a traditional wildflower meadow. They are extremely rare. Most of those lucky enough to have seen one will have seen a 'modern' meadow created by a nature conservation organisation of some sort.

Even the traditional meadows were artificially created by man allowing his stock to graze the area — mowing the lawn!

Rabbits have an effect on the wildflower species (and even the insect life) which live in meadows. They were introduced by the Normans for hunting and eating. Initially kept in warrens, they escaped and their grazing has helped some wildflowers survive in conditions which they would otherwise have found difficult.

So why create a wildflower meadow and how will your small area help in the survival of these ancient meadows?

- There's the experience you will gain from creating your meadow, which you can pass on to other interested parties.

- The result can be breathtaking, and the more people who see this and realise what can be achieved, the more will become interested in wildflowers. Some may plant wildflowers, which in turn will create more demand for seeds, more grown to fulfil the demand — more meadows, more seeds, more jobs!

- You will also create a bank of wildflower seeds which can be given to friends to create their own meadows. Some of these people may be in a position to influence local authorities, parks and gardens, councillors, etc., to establish wildflower meadows.

You may already, of course, possess a 'meadow' in your garden. It's called a lawn! With a little experimenting with the mower, or perhaps lifting a few turfs and sowing seeds, or planting pot-grown wildflowers in your lawn, everyone can create wildflower meadows!

THE LAZY MOWER'S MEADOW

Grass grows even when continually eaten or mowed, because a growing point at the base of each leaf blade produces new growth even when the leaf blade above is destroyed.

Unless you have a bowling green lawn, with regularly fed grass and weed killers destroying everything else, then you will already have some wildflowers in your lawn.

These will have evolved using different survival strategies to cope with continuous grazing by stock (or mowing by man), such as growing their leaves almost flat on the ground, known as rosettes, or living for years without flowering, or sending out runners which creep along through your lawn.

Some such wild flowers are yarrow, black medick, buttercups, self heal, daisies, clover and plantains — all common lawn 'weeds'. By leaving your lawn mower in the shed for a while just watch some of these flowers grow and bloom.

You can then cut the lawn again, on a high setting, cutting the grass and deheading the daisies and self heal. Then leave for another few days and this cycle can be repeated.

Not cutting shortly after these flowers have bloomed will cause the grasses to grow and eventually shade many lawn weeds out and they will die.

Leaving the mower in the shed for a slightly longer period will encourage the clover to flower, followed by yarrow. Pick four or five fresh yarrow leaves, wash them and place in a cup, pour on boiling water, leave for five minutes, add a little lemon juice and honey, sip and enjoy a lazy afternoon gazing at your lawn!

If you really **must** mow the lawn then try leaving little wildflower 'islands' uncut in a sea of green grass. Then make your drink, you'll have earned it!

Experiment by leaving some areas for longer periods. If you don't like the result simply cut the grass.

However, this is a flowering lawn and not a meadow. To introduce wildflowers cut out small turfs of grass and plant established, well-rooted, pot-grown wildflowers, then keep them well watered.

To help them compete against the established sward give each plant a little 5-6 cms black plastic collar mulch and cover this with some cut grass. This will pay dividends even though it may look a little unsightly. Once established and growing the collar can be removed.

This is best done on lawns which do not contain the vigorous rye grasses commonly grown in lawns for their toughness and durability.

Remember that wildflowers do not need feeding but lawn grasses do. By reducing the fertility of your soil you give wildflowers a better chance to compete with the grasses in your lawn. So remove any clippings and put them onto the compost heap.

A magnificent meadow or a low-cut lawn!

AN ANNUAL CORNFIELD MEADOW

A cornfield meadow can be a spectacular sight even if the area is only a two metre square. It requires little preparation or management — and all for the cost of a few packets of wildflower seeds.

Either purchase seed packets mixed for a cornfield meadow, or buy individual packets of the required species: corn cockle, cornflower, corn marigold, corn poppy, and perhaps scentless mayweed. Some mixtures may contain bearded wheat or barley, which can help to produce an authentic wild meadow.

Whilst other meadows you could plant contain many perennial plants, and consequently may take longer to establish, this meadow can exist made up entirely of annual plants grown from seed.

An annual cornfield meadow can be sown to give a quick result on land which is temporarily vacant prior to further development. For breathtaking beauty they are best planted in full sun in soil which is not prone to waterlogging and has low fertility.

Many of these flowers are extremely rare due to 'efficient' chemical weed control.

These plants are easily grown from seed and, being annuals, are best sown in their flowering position. The seeds need to come into contact with **bare** soil so that after germination they can grow happily in it. Scattering seeds on an established lawn is a waste of money.

To plant such a meadow on an existing lawn you either have to kill the grass or cut and remove turf. An efficient way of killing grass and weeds is to use an old carpet as a mulch.

If this vexes your partner, place the carpet the right way up and hoover it weekly! Alternatively, cover it with cocoa shells and benefit from that gorgeous chocolate smell. Keep your dog off it though — chocolate may not agree with him. Other coverings may also be used.

Do not use a foam-backed carpet as the foam is left in your soil as tiny, dust-like pieces. If you cover the carpet with a mulch it may rot quicker as this will keep it constantly damp.

Black plastic has the same effect but the ground will be very dry after a season and the carpet looks better! To be totally effective it has to be down for a **full** growing season. Leaving it down from March until September will eradicate even the most persistent weeds.

Removing the carpet for a couple of weeks prior to sowing will allow weed seeds to germinate. Then replace it and leave for another week, or hoe, dig or hand weed the weeds to leave a completely weed-free area ready for the next stage.

Do not use a rotavator as this will churn up numerous weed seeds which are just waiting for the right conditions to germinate.

If you (or your partner) don't like the carpet method (covered or not) then cut out and remove grass turfs, cutting pieces of a manageable size to carry away on a spade. They can be heavy if cut too large.

Each cut turf should be about 5-6 cms thick. By removing this fertile top soil the fertility of the soil is reduced, so making it more suitable for the needs of the wildflowers you are to sow.

To prevent grasses such as couch grass and weeds from invading your new cornfield meadow from the adjoining lawn, dig a trench between the two areas, 15 cms deep and 5 cms wide.

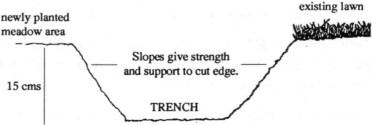

Remove any cut grass from the newly-planted area as it may smother young seedlings and add fertility to the soil.

SOIL PREPARATION AND SOWING

If you took the turf from your existing lawn there will be no need to remove the top 5 to 6 cms of topsoil; if not remove this soil. Enriched soil encourages the more aggressive weed and grass species to the detriment of your wildflowers, which are as yet still seeds. For cornfield annuals the poorer the soil the better the results.

The rich soil can be put to better use elsewhere in the garden and the turf, if stacked upside down for a year, will produce a friable loam.

You will now have a completely weed-free area of bare soil into which to sow your seeds. Remove stones and rake the area, to produce a fine level tilth. If the soil is too wet (wet enough to stick to your rake or boots) then delay until it's a little drier.

Divide your plot into equal areas, using rope, string or runner bean poles laid on the bare earth. Divide your seed mixtures into the same number of areas, keeping a small amount aside. (See below.) Soak the soil using a **fine** rose.

Mix seeds with a few handfuls of **dry** horticultural sand (damp sand tends to stick to itself) and scatter the mixture as evenly as possible. This allows you to see where you have actually sown and spreads the seeds further.

Sowing up and down first, then across (at right angles) will give a more even spread and distribution of seed.

Keep some seeds and sow them in modules to overwinter outside. These plants resent root disturbance, so use modules or pots and not a seed tray, which would mean pricking out prior to planting.

This tactic is useful as, when the seeds sown in situ germinate, any bare areas of soil can be filled by the module-grown plants, to produce a more even spread of flowers. These also act as an insurance in case seed germination is poor.

If you are sowing a grass mixture **and** wildflower seeds onto the same area, sow the grass seeds first and rake them into the soil, then the wildflower seeds, which only need to come into contact with the soil.

Do not rake once the wildflower seeds are sown. Poppies especially need light to germinate. Lightly tread in the seeds or use a roller if you have one. Sowing the seeds in Autumn produces earlier and larger flowers than a Spring sowing, by up to a month.

For best results, poppies need a period of cold before germination, which they would have with an Autumn sowing. If sown in Spring mix the seeds with damp horticultural sand and place in the fridge for two months, then mix with the other seeds as described.

corn cockle

This type of meadow depends upon soil disturbance. In theory, by disturbing the soil every Autumn the seeds will grow again to produce the same effect year after year. In practice, some annuals start to dominate the area — corn cockle especially, which germinates readily and early.

Other weeds and grasses also invade the area and set their seeds, so that after a few years the area becomes unbalanced and dominated by the corn cockle and unwanted weeds. It is then best to dig the area over and start the process again using your stock of seeds.

Every Autumn remove **all** vegetation from your cornfield patch (to remove fertility as the matter breaks down). Shake some seed heads over the area (after digging, raking and treading), then collect the remaining seeds to grow in modules and plugs as previously described.

A SPRING OR SUMMER MEADOW?

Both meadows will depend upon what flowers are planted, plus when **and** how often they are cut. Again, specialist seed companies can supply seeds for either meadow and will select the species to suit your soil type.

If starting with a bare patch of soil, seeds are best. Use the carpet method. Both types of meadow will contain perennials and are best planted with a blend of slow-growing grasses, to enable the seeds to germinate and grow without the competition of fast-growing grass.

The success or failure of this type of meadow, grown from seed, will depend on the variety of grasses blended with the wildflowers. A reputable seedsman can supply the right mixture.

Because of the cutting routine of a spring meadow, spring flowering bulbs such as wild daffodils can be planted in it once established.

WILDFLOWER SEEDS

What a typical mixture from a seedsman may contain.

Spring and Early Summer	Late Summer
common and ox-eye daisy	ox-eye daisy
ragged robin	greater and lesser knapweed
cowslip	field scabious
self heal	self heal
germander speedwell	wild carrot
red or white clover	yarrow
cat's ear	goatsbeard
meadow and bulbous buttercup	lady's bedstraw

CUTTING A WILDFLOWER MEADOW

As stated earlier, the cutting routine will determine which flowers actually flower and when. All cuttings should be removed to avoid fertility build-up and denial of light to the developing wildflowers.

With newly planted or sown areas especially, ensure that the blades are sharp. If not, they may tend to pull out or uproot any young seedlings. Tread the ground lightly before and after the first mowing to help consolidate the earth around the young seedlings.

In the first year of both types of meadow, allowing the flowers to establish themselves is vital. Cutting the grass to about 5 cms when it reaches a height of about 9 cms will ensure that light reaches the small seedlings but they don't get swamped by grasses.

This rather labour intensive, close attention to detail is vital for the wildflowers to become established. However, it is only required in the first year and you will reap huge rewards in the future.

Once established a spring meadow should be cut to about 5 cms in the Autumn, then left untouched until the flowers have flowered and set seed, usually by mid-July. It can then be cut regularly with its last cut in the Autumn.

The late summer meadow, **once established,** should be cut to about 5 cms at the start of the growing season and then left to flower and set seed, before being cut again in late September. A pre-winter cut to 5 cms can be given later in the season.

After flowering, leave the seed heads and stems in place for a day or two to allow them to shed their seeds before removal. As with the cornfield meadow, shaking some seed over the planted area and saving others to sow and transplant next Spring can pay dividends.

Part Seven

PONDS

WHY HAVE A POND?

A pond is probably the most effective and important wildlife mini-habitat you can create in your garden. An oasis of life is created in, on and around a pond and it is also used by passers-by to drink from or to bathe in.

In pond water there exists a complex life chain of predators, decomposers, herbivores, carnivores, parasites, worms, microscopic life and plant life.

Like many natural features of the past ponds are disappearing at an alarming rate. Pollution, drainage, natural drying out, being filled in, overgrowth and mismanagement are some reasons for their decline.

The pond does not hold the same importance today as it did when it was a vital part of village life, providing water for people to drink, cook and wash in, as well as a watering hole for cattle. There was no tap-water then. The village pond was also essential for putting out fires before fire tenders with water tanks were invented.

A pond has many uses for many wildlife species. For flatworms, water fleas and water snails it is a permanent home. For dragonflies and diving beetles it is a temporary home. For frogs and toads it is a breeding ground. Others just visit it. Birds, wasps and hedgehogs drink from it. Your dog may well swim in it — hopefully not if it's a flexible liner! And you will lose yourself as you gaze into it!

The following pages cover a few points worth considering before creating this important wildlife feature.

SIZE MATTERS!

Without doubt the bigger the pond the better. More wildlife is found in larger ponds, which can support more plant life too — essential for a healthy, thriving pond.

Competition for food is intense in a smaller pond and consequently there will be fewer survivors.

Small ponds tend to warm up quickly, especially if they are shallow. They can then often become too warm for wildlife, the water will evaporate at a quicker rate and algal blooms will grow faster.

Topping up your pond with cold tapwater means dramatic fluctuating temperatures. The more stable your pond's temperature the more stable its environment will become.

Tap-water contains nutrients which will encourage algal blooms and pondweed to thrive, will choke out other wildlife and exclude sunlight from the lower levels.

Plants produce oxygen from sunlight in the daytime and carbon dioxide in the evening. Too much pondweed in a small pond can quickly upset the natural balance between oxygen produced, oxygen used by wildlife and the build-up of carbon dioxide in the evening.

A small pond can totally freeze in Winter, killing any wildlife over-wintering in it, as can be seen in early Spring when dead frogs float to the top, having been either frozen or suffocated by trapped gases.

A good minimum size is about 4.5 square metres, with sides perhaps of 3 x 1.5 metres. To prevent the pond freezing completely the minimum depth should be at least 65 cms. This allows wildlife to seek refuge in it on hot days, as the deeper water will stay cool.

However, even a small tub filled with water can support some pond plants and maybe even some wildlife.

SITE

The siting of your pond is very important. Have a look at a pond which is completely shaded by trees and bushes, then look at a pond which receives sunshine and see for yourself which one has the most wildlife and which looks (and often smells!) the healthier.

If making your pond in Winter, consider the shade which will be cast by trees when in full leaf. An open, sunny aspect is best. Some shade can be given by planting floating plants and taller emergent plants on the **southern** aspect of the pond.

If trees are already established, and your pond has to be nearby, then site it to the south of them.

A pond sited so that it receives maximum sunshine literally teems with wildlife. The cooler temperature of a shaded pond can actually inhibit the growth of plants and wildlife, such as tadpoles. And shade can dictate which plants will grow successfully.

Also consider whether your pond will receive any pollution from chemical run-off from neighbouring gardens or fields. And are there any underground pipes or cables in the vicinity?

Trees shed leaves, which sink to the bottom and can smother lower plant life. Rotting leaves and twigs give off toxic gases as they decompose and eventually turn to slimy mud. Trees have roots. Will they impede or puncture your pond liner?

Open sited ponds away from trees require less clearing out of mud and debris — a disturbance which is potentially damaging to wildlife and plants, and is messy work too!

Is the site level? One temptation may be to site your pond in a natural hollow which collects water. In Winter these areas can collect a large volume of water. Pond liners have been known to float in their dug-outs, lifted by this seasonal volume of water.

Avoid waterlogged areas and digging below the natural water table as your feet will be wet and your spade will be extremely heavy! Late Winter is a good time to dig out a trial 60 cm trench to check the water table.

Consider what distance from your water source (for filling and topping up) your pond is to be sited? What distance will it be from your house too? Do you want to view it from the window or patio, or hide it at the bottom of the garden? — which would be a shame!

If you are thinking of hiring a digger to dig out a very large pond, has it access to your chosen site?

What will you do with the excavated soil? How far will you have to carry it? You can use the spoil to build a bank on one side of your pond, helping to shelter it from the prevailing north and east winds.

 This bank, if made on the north and east of the pond would be an ideal area in which to plant flowers to attract butterflies, especially the south facing bank, which would be sheltered and in continual sunlight — ideal butterfly conditions.

Giving your pond shelter from the wind also helps to reduce water evaporation. Wind tends to cool and often disturb the water surface. A cooler pond is more likely to freeze faster, more often and to a greater depth than a warmer, sheltered pond.

SHAPE

An irregular shape looks more natural and has a longer edge. Sharp corners cause unnatural creases in pond liners. Gentle curves are easier to make.

Provide shallow margins. Frogs prefer to lay their eggs in such areas, rather than in the deeper, cooler areas of the pond, as they warm up faster and encourage tadpole growth.

A gently sloping shingle or pebble 'beach' allows access to and from the pond for wildlife, and also allows birds to drink and bathe.

Use a rope, canes, hosepipe or string to mark out the shape of your pond. Walk around it; view it from different places and angles; go upstairs if need be and look down. You must be completely satisfied with your new pond's shape and position before starting work.

Ask the opinion of your partner. Much hard work lies ahead and you don't want to dig it out twice because the shape or site is wrong.

Avoid steep or vertical sides. Hedgehogs and birds will drown if the sides of a pond are too steep for them to clamber out.

Provide shelves at different heights, in order to have plants in pots or on shelves with raised lips. Different plants prefer different depths of water so the shelves can give you a larger choice of plants.

A saucer-shaped pond allows ice to slide up and down easily as it expands and contracts. Steep-sided walls are under considerable pressure from expanding ice, especially in concrete ponds.

A hard-standing viewing area is best sited opposite the sun, that is, along the north, east or west side of your pond. Otherwise your shadow will cast shade as you look down. Sunglasses will help to eliminate glare from the water.

EDGING

This can make a pond look natural or unnatural. Include
diverse edging material as different species will use the
edges for different purposes, for example frogs for sun
basking and dragonflies for emerging from the pond.

Rocks can hide the liner. Sandstone soaks up water, which then
encourages mosses to grow on it. Frogs sunbathe on stones and hide
under them when danger approaches.

Paving stones provide a firm footing for tiny feet — and larger feet
too! They make a good viewing platform and encourage observers

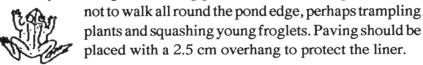
not to walk all round the pond edge, perhaps trampling
plants and squashing young froglets. Paving should be
placed with a 2.5 cm overhang to protect the liner.

Leave a gap between paving stones, in which to place soil and plant
flowers. Depending on the size of your pond, put a paving stone on
the opposite bank too. It will enable you to put a plank across the pond
when weeding or doing maintenance work in the middle.

Shingle or pebbled edges should be gently sloping. Heavier stones
further into the pond and around the outside of the 'beach' area will
keep lighter, smaller ones from being washed into deeper areas.

Logs make a good habitat and natural edge, and silver birch looks
particularly attractive as the bark remains long after the wood has
rotted. It is also easily replaced.

Sods of grass look natural and effective. However, if continually
trampled they may soon break up, after which the grass will grow into
the water and act as a wick, evaporating the water much faster.

Ensure no couch grass is in the turf as it can penetrate and puncture
liners, even butyl ones.

diving beetle

Do not use the turf if you regularly feed your lawn with chemical fertilisers or weed killers. They may leach into the pond, increasing nutrients and harming plants and wildlife.

Try to include a transitional zone as one of your edges. Wildlife will use this to pass to and from the pond. A pond completely surrounded by bricks or paving makes wildlife, such as froglets, easy prey when caught on such edging by birds and cats.

A nylon onion bag, stuffed with pebbles, can act as a dam if placed on a gently sloping shelf, back-filled with soil and planted up with such plants as creeping jenny or ragged robin. Even water mint likes growing in this type of area, which becomes a mini-marsh or bog.

A PRE-MOULDED POND

Most people either choose to buy a pre-moulded pond or a liner. Puddling clay and bentonite (which is used to build reservoirs) can be used to make ponds, but for most people the following are easily bought and readily available:

fibreglass or plastic pre-moulded ponds - concrete

polythene - PVC sheeting or butyl.

Pre-moulded and shaped pools come in a variety of plastics and fibreglass but you have no choice as to your pond's shape and they are usually on the small side, even though they look enormous when standing on their ends in garden centres!

Having steep and slippery sides makes it difficult for wildlife to get into the pond to drink and bathe, and to get out. To assist them, artificial bridges have to be made, such as high piles of logs or stones.

The hole dug needs to accommodate a pre-moulded pond precisely, which may mean digging a larger hole, then back filling it after fitting the pond. Laying these ponds on a cushion of sand is recommended.

When the water freezes the pressures and stresses of the ice can force the walls outwards. If there is a gap between the wall and the soil which reinforces it the walls sometimes crack.

Edging these ponds, especially if you wish them to look natural, can be difficult and your choices are very limited. A transitional zone or bog/marsh area can only be achieved by adding a separate liner next to your rigid pond. So why not just buy a liner and incorporate the bog area within the same liner?

A CONCRETE POND

These are difficult to make, are very labour intensive and need to be made in **one** day, in good weather! A steel/wire cage to reinforce the concrete should be used, on top of a firm foundation of rocks or stones. If you've not worked with concrete before you may wish to think again!

A 10 cm thickness can make a very strong structure but stresses by ice in Winter can crack or damage it, especially if it has steep or vertical sides. Subsidence and tree roots can cause problems too and these ponds do not look very natural.

Chemicals in the concrete can be harmful to wildlife and the pond should not be planted up, or wildlife added, until these have dissipated. After filling the pond leave the water for a few days before emptying it out, scrubbing both walls and base, refilling the pond and leaving it for a few more days. Then repeat the process.

The water needs to be changed several times and then left to season prior to any planting up. This could take up to a month of emptying and refilling again before plants and wildlife are introduced.

pond skater

FLEXIBLE LINERS

These can be superb ponds for wildlife and offer the widest choice in shape and size. With careful planning given to the pond edge and any surplus liner, natural looking ponds can be made relatively easily.

Polythene comes in various thicknesses and a 1,000 gauge is quite strong. 'Visqueen', a builders' polythene, will also make a successful pond, especially the 1,500 gauge designed for lining reservoirs.

Any exposure to the sun's harmful ultra-violet rays will turn polythene brittle, drastically reducing the life expectancy of both pond and wildlife. So make sure the polythene is completely covered with a layer of soil 10 cms deep.

Polythene can be used successfully for making bog/marsh areas too, as they are completely buried by soil. It is cheaper than butyl which, if used, makes a bog/marsh area much more expensive.

However, polythene does not have the elasticity or stretchability which both PVC and butyl possess, but leaving it out in the warm sunlight prior to fitting should make it more manageable.

PVC is more hard wearing than polythene and consequently more expensive. It can also be purchased with a tough nylon reinforcing mesh woven into it.

A butyl liner is a better, but more expensive option. It is a thick, heavy duty, rubber-like liner which will last for many years. If you want to enlarge your pond, simple kits and extension pieces can be easily bought, making this a relatively simple process.

All flexible liners are prone to damage by such things as sharp stones, dogs' claws and garden forks. Take particular care with the edges as these are more prone to punctures. If you have to stand in your pond wear soft-soled shoes and stand on a piece of carpet.

MAKING A POND WITH A BUTYL LINER

Materials:

One 25 cm and several 10 cm wooden pegs, and a plank of wood.

Mallet, rake, spade, plasterer's trowel, rope/hosepipe/string.

Spirit level, tape measure, gloves and a wheelbarrow.

Underliner of polyester matting. (Carpet and folded newspaper can be used but they soon rot.)

Builders' sand, pebbles and pea gravel.

Tea, coffee and cakes for the volunteers!

It makes life easier if the chosen site is reasonably level, as having the edges of your pond level will dictate whether you have a pond or a waterfall, as the water pours out at the pond's lowest point!

Mark out your pond (having chosen the site well), with canes, rope or hosepipe, or draw the shape using dry sand in a bottle.

Clear the area of vegetation around the perimeter, removing shrub and bramble roots or, if sited in a lawn, cut and remove the turf. Make sure this is cleared to outside your pond marker(s) and put it to one side for possible use as an edging later.

Using your eye, find the lowest level of the pond's perimeter and mark it using one of the wooden pegs. Hammer this into the ground so that the top is exactly level with the soil. This peg (1) is your marker peg.

Immediately outside this area is the best site to make your bog/marsh garden as any excess water will tend to flow into it.

Lay a plank of wood on top of the marker peg and across the ground towards the centre of the pond. Cut out a channel of soil under the plank, cutting towards the centre of the pond. In this channel, and at the centre of the pond, hammer in the 25 cm peg (the pivot peg) and ensure it protrudes well above peg 1 to allow for any adjustment.

Lay the plank across from peg 1 to the pivot peg, using the spirit level to check it is level. Hammer home the pivot peg, ensuring that the plank stays level as it bridges from peg 1 to the pivot peg.

The pivot peg is used to determine the level of the rest of the perimeter by rotating the plank from the centre to the perimeter and inserting pegs along this, level to the centre. For stability, you could use a long screw to secure the plank to the pivot peg, ensuring it can move freely as it rotates, like a finger on a clock.

As with peg 1, you may have to dig a channel for the plank to lie flat on the ground before the next peg is hammered home at the perimeter. This soil would have to be removed anyway, so this does not cause any extra work.

Always place the spirit level on top of the plank prior to hammering home a peg to make sure the **plank** is level. Do **not** hammer the peg home to ground level.

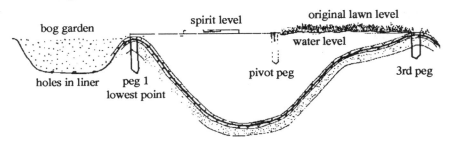

Outline of completed pond prior to soil removal.

In some areas you may have to use soil to build up the edge, bringing it **up** to the level of the top of the peg and along to the level of the top of its neighbouring peg.

Rotate the plank from the pivot peg and hammer home pegs until the full perimeter is marked out at approximately every 60 cms.

To double check the edge is level, place the plank and spirit level across a peg to its neighbour.

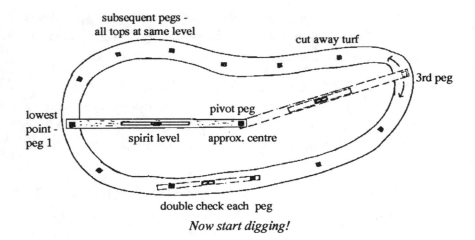

Now start digging!

You can omit shelves when digging but aquatics can be planted in baskets on top of these. This is worth bearing in mind because rampant plants can be kept in check with the basket method.

Remember to dig a sloping beach and, for a bog/marsh area, dig a little channel at the lowest point of the pond, into which overflow water will drain.

Once your hole is dug may be a good time to measure the pond before buying a liner! Lay a piece of rope or string along its full length and the same at its widest stretch, remembering to allow for an edging 'overhang' and your chosen edging design.

The bog/marsh area does not require the more expensive butyl liner and polythene or PVC can be used here. Puncture it in a few places or it will simply fill up and stagnate. There are a wide choice of plants available for this area. It will need topping up with water in the Summer and tap-water can be used — but a water butt is better.

Once the pond is dug to the correct depth (at least 76 cms) you **have** to remove all the stones, roots and sharp objects from the soil. Rake the soil over to reveal hidden objects just under the soil surface, then firm down all the sides and the bottom.

Dampen the builders' sand and, with a trowel, firmly plaster it over all the soil surface to a depth of 3 cms if using the custom-made underliner, or 5 cms if using old carpets — as many as possible. Mould the liner into the pond's shape. Remove all wooden pegs.

Roll the pond liner up and place it along the longest edge of the pond. Unroll it, leaving enough liner to cut to shape and enough to finish off with your particular choice of edging, whether plants or paving.

Secure the rolled part of the liner with bricks or heavy stones and then unroll the rest of the liner over the hole, shaping if necessary. Be aware of the danger of puncturing the liner if you have to step into it to unfold a crease.

If you can afford the extra money, put another underliner on **top** of the pond liner. This precaution is in case the liner is damaged from above.

underliner
pond liner
underliner
sand

Secure the whole liner with bricks or stones on its outer edge and fill the pond up with water. The weight of the water will mould the liner to shape and gradually lift the stones as the pond fills up.

Use bricks or large stones to hold the liner in place. Fill it up slowly, allowing the weight of the water to take the slack up gradually.

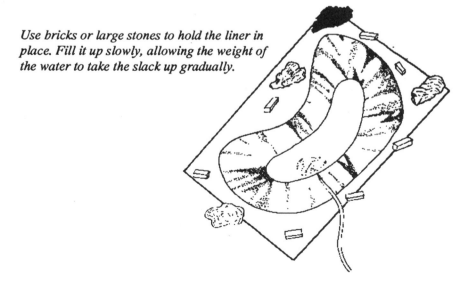

Once filled, sieve some **subsoil** into the pond. (Topsoil would be richer in nutrients and may encourage algal blooms.) Then add some sieved mud from an established pond. The water will look murky for a few days and as it clears you can see if you need to add more soil to any exposed section of liner. Polythene and PVC will require more soil depth than butyl.

Make your 'beach' area with gravel and larger pebbles. Finish off cutting the edge of the liner, adding your edging material, for example turf, and bury the remaining edge of the liner 8 cms into the surrounding soil.

Do not introduce plants or wildlife for at least ten days.

LEAKS

Dealing with leaks depends on the type of material from which your pond is constructed. Although repair kits are obtainable for the pond liners mentioned earlier, polythene liners may well have become brittle and any repairs would just be delaying the inevitable. Buy a butyl liner and make a bigger, better pond!

If your butyl pond is leaking, instead of patching it up why not go the whole hog and extend it? A little more digging and larger 'patches' of butyl are all that is needed. It could well mean less lawn to cut!

Try to keep at least a small part of your pond ice-free in Winter. This allows gases to escape which, potentially, could harm the pond's wildlife as well as its exchange of oxygen.

Boiling water, or placing a saucepan of hot water on top of the ice, will help here. Make sure you catch the pan before it sinks to the bottom though! That water's cold!

MANAGEMENT AND MAINTENANCE

The success of a pond can be determined by its siting and planting. The plants will have to be managed to benefit wildlife.

Minerals/nutrients are the key to a successful pond. Soil, minerals from tap water, decomposing plant/animal material and sunlight, add nutrients, an excess of which encourages algal blooms (phytoplankton) which feed on the nutrients.

The two most common and problematic algal blooms which occur in ponds are the free floating types (giving the appearance of pea soup) and the filamentous types (causing blanket weed).

Controlling algal blooms can be achieved by:

- **reducing the available food.** All plants in the pond will compete for the nutrients (food) in it. By introducing submerged and floating aquatic plants you will increase competition for the available food.

- **topping up water.** Use rainwater, not mineral-enriched tap-water to top up your pond. If you can only use tap-water then a little and often is the best practice. Let it stand for 48 hours before using it.

- **reducing nutrients.** Ensure that no chemical fertilisers leach into your pond from your garden or surrounding areas. Adding soil adds nutrients to the pond. Use soil/mud from an established pond. Remove decomposing plant and animal matter. Removing weed growth reduces nutrients locked up in the plants.

- **denying direct sunlight.** Algal blooms need sunlight. Make sure that more than a third of your pond's surface is covered with floating aquatics and also plant submerged aquatics. The shade these plants cast will deny sunlight to the algal blooms.

- **feeding particular plants.** Waterlilies are particularly hungry for nutrients and may well need extra feeding. By planting them in plastic baskets, and buying **slow release** fertilisers from specialist aquatic plant dealers, you will feed the lily and not allow fertilisers to leach out to feed other plants, including algae.

- **removing blanket weed.** Do this with a stick or cane. Use a winding motion, then drag it out — taking the nutrients with it.

- **adding natural predators.** Algae is preyed upon by daphnia and cyclops, commonly known as water fleas (zooplankton).

  daphne (water flea)

- **adding barley straw.** This has a two-fold effect on algae. As it rots down it causes the algae to coagulate and sink to the bottom. The lignin in the straw also breaks down, producing chemicals which naturally inhibit and affect the algae's reproductive cycle. Barley straw pads are available for garden ponds and are best used in early Spring, then again in Autumn. (See Appendix for stockists.)

When removing weed from your pond, give any wildlife entangled in it a chance to escape by either leaving the weed next to the pond for a while, moving it to a shallow beach area, or putting it into a bucket and later pouring the water and wildlife back into the pond. Then compost the weeds.

Blanket weed especially can be very tough and its strands can imprison small wildlife. Cutting the strands into smaller pieces, stacking them next to the pond, then removing the top layers first and gradually working your way down over a few days if necessary, will make it easier for wildlife to escape and return to the pond.

Although chemical solutions are available from aquatic shops to control algae, and appear to work initially, they do not deal with the underlying, long-term problem. Avoid chemicals. They may also have an adverse effect on your pond life.

In Autumn, netting the pond can prevent leaves, twigs, fruit and other objects falling into, then rotting in the pond, using up valuable oxygen and making poisonous gases.

Bloodworms and rat-tailed maggots (a hoverfly's larvae which use their long tails to breathe) live in the foul, stagnant and polluted water caused by rotting vegetation, upon which they feed.

An abundance of them is an indicator that the balance in your pond is awry and the rotting vegetation and debris on the bottom probably needs clearing out.

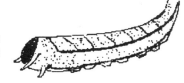

A rat tailed maggot, which breathes through its large, 'snorkel' tail, lives in stagnant water and feeds on rotting vegetation.

The removal of all dead leaves and dead pond vegetation, twigs, rampant weed growth and any dead animals or birds, as soon as any of these appear, will help to alleviate the problem. It may also avert the need for a major pond clearance of the mud and debris lying on the bottom and check the pollution from decaying matter.

If you do have to clear out your pond there are arguments for and against whether to do it in Spring or Autumn. Some wildlife and plants will be adversely affected at any time of year.

Early Spring will at least enable plantlife to regrow rapidly as Summer approaches, and most wildlife will not have laid their eggs.

A clearance in Autumn is when plants have stopped growing and most wildlife too. It is also a good time to check any plastic plant baskets for splits and renew them.

If floating duckweed becomes a problem simply scoop it off the pond's surface and leave it near the shingle beach. This may have to be done daily, especially in the summer months.

PLANTING

A pond is a self-contained ecosystem in which plants play a vital part, providing food and oxygen, shelter and shade, breeding places and 'bridges' from the aquatic world to our own, for such creatures as damsel and dragonflies.

Save yourself money and obtain your plants from the well established ponds of friends. Avoid the risk of introducing non-native and potentially problematic species. Buy, or borrow from the library, a good reference book for pond plant identification and planting up.

A healthy pond has achieved the right balance between its plants and wildlife.

Free Floating Plants — frogbit, water soldier, water hawthorn. These need no planting

Oxygenators — curly pondweed, hornwort, water milfoil, water starwort.

Hornwort thrown into the pond will survive without being planted in the soil. All the others need planting in soil or baskets.

Hornwort, looking like a bottlewasher with its whorled leaves, is an excellent, natural oxygenator.

Emergent/Marginal Plants — arrowhead, bog bean, brooklime, flowering rush, lesser reedmace, water forget-me-nots, water mint.

Bog/Marsh Plants — creeping jenny, *devil's bit scabious, *hemp agrimony, *lady's smock, marsh marigold, meadow sweet, *purple loosestrife, ragged robin, *water mint.

Many of these are pretty flowers and those starred (*) have the added bonus of being attractive to bees and some butterflies.

Floating Plants with Rooted Bases — broad leaf pondweed, water crowsfoot, water lilies.

PLANTS TO AVOID

As with many aspects of wildlife gardening, native is best. However, there are a few exceptions here, especially with your choice of water lilies. Buy these from a specialist water lily grower and seek advice about which species is best suited to your pond. (Stockists are listed in the Appendix.)

Although beautiful in its own way, our native yellow and white flowering waterlily is aggressive and will quickly out-compete and smother other plants. It is best only planted in the largest and deepest ponds, and avoided if you have a small one. Other native, floating plants are available.

The same can be said of other native plants, such as greater spearwort and bulrush. Smaller, named varieties may be obtainable from specialist aquatic shops.

The following non-native, introduced species are very aggressive, will quickly choke out any native plant species you may already have in your pond and may well over-colonise it. They are generally sold using their Latin names:

> water fern (azolla filiculloides)
>
> Canadian pond weed (elodea canadensis)
>
> New Zealand water stonecrop (crassula helmsii).

FROGS, TOADS AND NEWTS

Do not take frogs, toads and other amphibians, nor their spawn, from the wild. This may be illegal anyway. Frogs have been suffering from a debilitating disease called 'red leg'. You could help this to spread by taking infected adults. Wild populations are struggling enough.

Instead, contact your local Wildlife Trust who will be only too happy to supply you either with the spawn itself or a contact from whom you can collect it. Alternatively, ask a neighbour or friend, who may already have a pond full of it.

Frogs and toads can take up to three years to reach breeding maturity. To establish a viable breeding population in your pond introduce spawn over a three year period.

The changing from spawn to froglet generally takes 3+ months. If, by the end of the tenth week you notice that the tadpoles' hind legs are not fully grown they are late developers! This may be due to overcrowding, lack of food, too much shade or too cool water.

Add a few drops of iodine into the pond. Elements in it are used by the tadpoles and their metamorphosis will speed up.

Frog spawn and tadpoles have a hard time whilst in the pond. If you see spawn which is turning grey or white then it has not been fertilised and will rot in the pond.

Those which have been fertilised have to run the gauntlet of being eaten by numerous predators, such as beetles, their larvae, damsel and dragonfly larvae, water scorpions and water-boatmen. Then there are the jam jar boys!

Some water-boatmen feast on tadpoles.

They also have to find enough food themselves. In the early stages boiled lettuce leaves can help. As they get older their food changes to meat. Chopped up worms are eagerly accepted, as are minced morsels. Remove all such food after a day as it will start to rot.

As they leave the pond small frogs are easy prey for birds and cats. And be careful when you mow the lawn, especially near the pond. Either cut the lawn around the pond regularly to discourage frogs from finding refuge there or, better still, don't mow round the pond at all, as many will find refuge in the longer, uncut grass. This area could also be used by wildlife as a corridor to another haven.

 Before they breed frogs have to find sites to overwinter for at least two consecutive Winters and, having survived those cold seasons, also have to avoid predators and find enough food to eat during the intervening periods. Not many tadpoles survive to become mature, breeding adults and that's why so much spawn is laid.

Frogs, toads and newts don't hibernate like hedgehogs. Instead, they fall into a state of torpor. Whilst in this state, even when underwater, a frog has the ability to 'breathe' through its skin. Hence the importance of your pond always having a frost-free air hole.

Provide overwintering sites by having log piles, mounds of stones or brushwood and small compost heaps in quiet areas of your garden.

Plants at the pond's edge will give young frogs, toads and newts a safer passage from pond to land, as well as providing shelter from the hot, dry sun and potential predators. These plants will also give dragon and damselflies something to use to climb out of the pond.

Take some frogspawn, water and pondweed from your pond and place it in a plastic bowl or fish tank. Keep it in a light, warm place out of direct sunlight and watch the tadpoles develop.

If you wish to study them until they turn into froglets place a partially submerged stone inside the container. In the later stages their developing lungs need to be able to breathe and rest, or they will drown. At this stage feed them ants or aphids.

These lucky tadpoles can be safely returned to an area near the pond, such as the 'beach'. Having escaped the carnage in the pond which will have decimated their brothers and sisters, they will stand a better chance of survival.

Whose egg it it anyway?
Frogs lay their eggs in large 'blobs', all clumped together to form seething masses. They favour the warmer, shallower areas of a pond, where many females may lay their eggs.

Toads lay theirs in slightly deeper water. They wrap a string of eggs, which looks like dotted toothpaste and can be a metre or more long, around submerged plants.

Newts use a different approach to egg laying as each egg is laid individually on the leaf of a submerged plant.

Spot the tadpole!
Frog tadpoles are brown with speckles of gold all over their body.

Toad tadpoles are much darker — almost black.

Newt tadpoles have large, feathery gills sticking up behind their heads like horns.

ATTRACTING OTHER WILDLIFE

You will not have much difficulty here! Wildlife will soon find your pond. Fish and pond wildlife do not mix. It may be interesting to watch your fish swim but there will be far more wildlife if there are no fish, making your pond potentially more interesting to watch!

Fish eat the smaller pond life, for instance daphnia, the predator of algae. Tadpoles are also easy prey. Keep your fish in a fish pond.

pond skater

You may be lucky enough to see pond skaters gliding over your pond's surface, using their deadly mouth parts to pierce such prey as flies unfortunate enough to fall in the water. Ten out of ten for style and grace!

The jet black whirlygig beetles are also fascinating as they move and spin along the surface like bumper cars which never bump!

You may also see bottle green, ant-like flies with white ensigns on their wings. These dance around flicking their wings, then walk up and down on water lilies in the hope of attracting a mate.

The singing of the birds, the buzzing of the bees, the skaters skimming over the surface and the dancing flies, what could be more delightful on a summer evening!

Part Eight

APPENDIX

ORGANISATIONS AND SUPPLIERS

Native Wildflower Seeds and Plants
Landlife Wild Flowers Ltd, The Old Police Station, Lark Lane, Liverpool, L17 8UU. *Tel:* 0151 728 7011
Naturescape, Little Orchard, Whatton in the Vale, Nottingham, NG13 9EP. *Tel:* 01949 51045
Mike Handyside Wild Flowers, 28 Woodlands Park, Allostock, Knutsford, WA16 9LG. *Tel:* 01565 722995

Wild Birds
RSPB, The Lodge, Sandy Bedfordshire, SG19 2DL.
Tel: 01767 80551
British Trust for Ornithology (BTO), The Nunnery, Thetford, Norfolk, IP24 2PU. *Tel:* 01842 750050

Bird Foods, Feeders, Next Boxes and Wildlife Accessories
(Mail Order Catalogues available)
C J Wild Bird Foods, The Rea, Upton Magna, Shrewsbury, SY4 4UB. *Tel:* 01743 709545
Jacobi Jayne & Company, Hawthorn Cottage, Maypole Heath, Canterbury, Kent, CT3 4LW. *Tel:* 01227 868388
Ernest Charles, Crediton, EX17 2YZ. *Tel:* 0800 731 6770
Barley Straw Pads, Green Ways Environmental Care, South End Farm, Ockham, Woking, Surrey, GU23 6PF. *Tel:* 01483 281392

Hedgehogs
British Hedgehog Preservation Society, Knowbury House, Knowbury, Ludlow, Shropshire, SY8 3LQ. *Tel:* 01584 890801

Bats
Bat Conservation Trust, 15 Cloisters House, 8 Battersea Park Road, London, SW8 4BG. *Tel:* 0171 627 2629

Organic Gardening — advice, research, seeds, pest control.
Henry Doubleday Research Association (HDRA), Ryton Gardens,
Ryton on Dunsmore, Coventry, CV8 3LG. *Tel:* 01203 303 517
The Good Gardeners Association, The Pinetum, Churcham,
Gloucester, GL2 8AD. *Tel:* 01452 750402

Organic Farming — advice and research.
The Soil Association, Bristol House, Victoria Street, Bristol,
BS1 6BY. *Tel:* 0117 929 0661

Native Trees and Shrubs from Seed
Alba Trees, Lower Winton, Gladsmuir, East Lothian, EH33 2AL.
Tel: 01620 825058
'Rootrainers' from Ronnash Ltd, Kersquarter, Kelso, Roxburghshire,
TD5 8HH. *Tel:* 01573 225757
Trees of Time and Place. *Helpline:* 0345 078 139
Tree Growing Kits from the Arid Lands Initiative
Tel: 01422 843 807
The Tree Council. *Tel:* 0171 828 9928
The Woodland Trust. *Tel:* 01476 581 111

Butterflies
Butterfly Conservation, PO Box 222, Dedham, Colchester, Essex,
CO7 6EY. *Tel:* 01206 322342

Wildflowers
Flora Locale, 36 Kingfisher Court, Hambridge Road, Newbury,
Berkshire, RG14 5SJ.
Plantlife — Natural History Museum, London, SW7 5BD

Water Plants and Liners
Stapeley Water Gardens, London Road, Nantwich, Cheshire,
CW5 7LH. *Tel:* 01270 628111

Frogspawn and Other Wildlife Advice
The Wildlife Trusts. *Tel:* 01522 544400

FURTHER READING

How to Make a Wildlife Garden by Chris Baines,
Elm Tree Books, 1985

The Living Garden by Michael Chinery, Dorling Kindersley, 1986

Creating a Wildlife Garden by Bob and Liz Gibbons, Hamlyn, 1988

The National Trust Book of Wildflower Gardening
by John Stephens, Dorling Kindersley, 1987

Organic Magazine.
A monthly magazine offering up-to-date information on all aspects
of organic gardening.
Details from PO Box 4, Wiveliscombe, Taunton, Somerset,
TA4 2QY. *Tel:* 01984 623998

In this series:
Organic Gardening by Ruth Jacobs

Alfresco Books,
7 Pineways, Appleton, Warrington, WA4 5EJ.
Fax/Tel: 01925 267503

List of titles published by *Alfresco Books* available on request.

ABOUT THE AUTHOR

George Pilkington runs a variety of practical, organic and wildlife gardening courses for the Workers Educational Association (WEA). Informative talks and advice to organisations throughout the North West are another speciality. He also advises schools and local authorities on environmental issues, and has led nature and conservation courses for the Field Studies Council.

While in the police force, George visited schools to demonstrate the human aspect of policing and to show how approachable a 'bobby' could be. Besides bringing insects in to show the children, he also took classes out on nature walks to see the wildlife of hedges, grew plants with the children, planted trees and, at one school, even constructed a pond.

Later, George decided to make a career of teaching adults, including those with special needs. With these he has recently created a nature reserve — planting hedges, growing trees from seed, developing wildflower meadows and making a large pond.

ragged robin